Christ Through Hazel Eyes

**30-DAY DEVOTIONAL
TRUE INSPIRATIONAL STORIES
HIGHLIGHTING JESUS IN EVERYDAY LIFE**

CHERI J BECH

Praise for *Christ Through Hazel Eyes*

"The articulate simplicity and heartwarming authenticity of Cheri Bech's writing will quickly make this devotional a favorite for many. From the first chapter, I found myself pulled in. Each one was both adventurous and encouraging! As a man, I never intended to read this devotional, but Cheri's life story made it interesting and relatable, and not just because I know her. (My father was her karate instructor for many years.) With a husband who was an outstanding NFL player and later a coach, and Cheri herself—a fiery, tough karate challenger who became an NFL cheerleader—her insights into life's ups and downs, victories and personal hardships, are nothing short of inspiring. Through it all, she discovered the secret to it all: Jesus. I encourage both men and women to take this devotional to heart—not just for spiritual growth, but to build a real, authentic relationship with the One who will never leave you or fail you: Jesus."

—Victor Marx (ATP Ministries)

"Each story is inviting and relatable. The Scripture references at the end of each chapter allow an opportunity for a deeper study, and the questions lead the reader to experience self-reflection in a straightforward and applicable way. I highly recommend this book to anyone looking to engage in practical spiritual growth."

—Kanika Evans

"*Christ Through Hazel Eyes* is a heartfelt and inspiring devotional that beautifully reflects God's presence, faithfulness, and miraculous work in our lives. Through touching stories of her own family's journey, Cheri Bech invites readers to see Christ's love and provision through her eyes, encouraging us to trust Him more deeply. This devotional is a blessing to anyone longing to experience the nearness of Christ and His hand in their everyday lives."

—Andrea Lende, Best-Selling Author and Speaker

PRAISE FOR CHRIST THROUGH HAZEL EYES

"As I read these stories and envision Christ through the beautiful hazel eyes of Cheri Bech, I am awestruck and grateful for my wonderful friend. Cheri's words are weighed and measured, piercing the heart of all who read this devotional book. The Scriptures and questions cause us to think more deeply into the heart of Jesus. One of the verses that Cheri chose is Psalm 34:8 (NASB), "Taste and see that the Lord is good; How blessed is the man who takes refuge in Him!" Cheri's heart's desire is obvious, that we might know and experience more of Jesus and see Him working in and through our lives every day!"

—Carol Weber

"*Christ Through Hazel Eyes.* Though the stories in these pages allow you the chance to see Christ throughout, Cheri has allowed me to see Christ within. Within her, within me, and within those around me. I pray she does the same for you as her hazel eyes take you on a journey of the unseen forces behind that which we all see. Cheri's outward and upward gaze shows us how to get out from behind our own eyes and see what God is doing in front of us. I pray this book blesses you as much as she has blessed me."

—Jessica Wuerffel

Copyright © 2024 by Cheri J. Bech

All rights reserved.

No portion of this book may be reproduced in any form without written permission from the publisher or author, except as permitted by U.S. copyright law.

Scripture quotations marked (CSB) are taken from the Christian Standard Bible. Copyright © 2017 by Holman Bible Publishers. Used by permission. Christian Standard Bible®, and CSB® are federally registered trademarks of Holman Bible Publishers, all rights reserved. Scripture quotations marked (ESV) are taken from the ESV® Bible (The Holy Bible, English Standard Version®). ESV® Text Edition: 2016. Copyright © 2001 by Crossway, a publishing ministry of Good News Publishers. The ESV® text has been reproduced in cooperation with and by permission of Good News Publishers. Unauthorized reproduction of this publication is prohibited. All rights reserved. Scripture quotations marked (NIV) are taken from THE HOLY BIBLE, NEW INTERNATIONAL VERSION®, NIV® Copyright © 1973, 1978, 1984, 2011 by Biblica, Inc.® Used by permission. All rights reserved worldwide. Scripture quotations marked (KJV) are taken from the King James Version. Scripture quotations marked (NLT) are taken from the *Holy Bible*, New Living Translation, copyright © 1996, 2004, 2015 by Tyndale House Foundation. Used by permission of Tyndale House Publishers, Inc., Carol Stream, Illinois 60188. All rights reserved.

ISBN: 978-1-962581-58-5
eISBN: 978-1-962581-59-2

Design: Ruth Hovsepian
Photos & Cover Image: From the author's private collection.

TIGER BECH

#7 St. Thomas More Cougars, Princeton Tigers

(7 to heaven)

You took one for the team. Now it's up to us to run the rest of the race with grit and endurance to make it safely "home." We will not fail. May Jesus be our light, and may heaven be our reward. Thank you for loving life, for loving us, and for never ceasing to give us your all. We love you and promise never to give up.

My nephew was taken in the attack in New Orleans in the early hours of New Year's Day, 2025. His passing left a significant impact on everyone who knew him, and we each recognize the life Tiger lived—tenacious, passionate, and full of love until his very last breath. His absence has brought much healing and unity to a hurting world. He led the way and would want us to fight each day and let love win. Our prayers remain with the victims' families and all those affected as they heal from this tragedy.

To Ryan Quigley, a survivor of the New Orleans attack: You were not only Tiger's teammate at Princeton but also his teammate in life. The torch has been passed to you. A piece of Tiger lives on in you, which is so clear to all of us. May God strengthen you every step of the way. You are family. We love you and are always cheering you on.

> "You intended to harm me, but God intended it for good to accomplish what is now being done, the saving of many lives."
>
> Genesis 50:20 (NIV)

GOD IS LOVE

Dedication

First and foremost, I dedicate this book to Jesus Christ, the Author of my life. Without Him, I am but dirt in the ground, and without His breath in my stories, they are just jumbled up, meaningless words on paper. Thank You, Jesus, for everything!

To my husband. As early as our dating days, I remember you tearing up as you read my birthday cards, not only the ones written to you, but also the ones written to others. I would read them to you to see if they sounded good, and you never failed to act as if I had just written the Declaration of Independence itself. Your constant encouragement has propelled me to become a confident author. I feel safe and free to explore every avenue God places before me, knowing you will support me wholeheartedly. You are the one who took me through avenues of my heart that I did not even know existed. Thank you for exemplifying and teaching me a characteristic of Christ by remaining *steadfast* in your love for me for close to three decades now. This love has spilled over onto our family with you being such a strong godly leader, ever-present father, and most gentle, loving daddy. Our four daughters *know* what they deserve in a husband because you have consistently and genuinely shown it to them every day of their lives by the way you love me. You have taught each of us that our voice matters. I am so honored to be your wife and blessed to love you throughout eternity.

Contents

Introduction	XIII
1. Nibble	1
2. The Bridge and The Bench	5
3. Front Yard Football to Sideline Cheer	9
4. Losing My Daddy	17
5. Forgiveness = Freedom	23
6. Mud	29
7. Save Me, Jesus!	33
8. Hands	37
9. Hearing	41
10. Put It Down	45
11. Pink Barbie Slipper	51
12. Seek	55
13. Turn Around	59
14. Crossroads	65
15. Pretty Please	71
16. Good Friday	75
17. Naked and Afraid	79
18. Shotgun Rider	85

19.	In Just A Little While	89
20.	Sink	95
21.	Down the Aisle	101
22.	Presence	107
23.	Waves	111
24.	Get Up and Go	115
25.	Calm	121
26.	Baby Bird Eggs	125
27.	Heavenly Hugs	131
28.	Farewells	135
29.	Counting	139
30.	The Tunnel	143
	Last Word for the Reader	147
	How This Book Was Birthed	149
	Acknowledgments	151
	About Cheri Bech	163

Christ Through Hazel Eyes

INTRODUCTION

Dear Friend,

The memories within these pages are moments throughout my life when God's presence has been unmistakable—times when I noticed His love wrapping around me, carrying me through both joyful and difficult seasons. These are moments I return to, again and again, to be reminded of His faithfulness.

What makes my stories special? Nothing. Nothing at all except for the mercy of God Almighty Himself. They're pieces of my life woven with grace, the same way your life is. I just felt led to share my stories with you, to help prompt the recognition of God's loving presence throughout your own journey. He's there, even in the moments that feel ordinary or insignificant, guiding you through valleys, lifting you, and leading you to mountaintops. And as you start to notice His presence, may you feel an ever-deepening courage to share your own story, to help another heart know the love of Christ.

I encourage you not to rush through the book but to read one story at a time, letting the Lord's presence seep into your soul, allowing His Word to become well-rooted within. As you journey through these pages, remember this promise:

"The Lord himself goes before you and will be with you; he will never leave you nor forsake you. Do not be afraid; do not be discouraged." Deuteronomy 31:8 (NIV)

In Christ,
Cheri

1

NIBBLE

WHEN WALKING INTO MY Maw Maw and Paw Paw's house, I was sure to find their dining room table covered with Bibles, devotionals, and books all scattered about. Most of the time, I entered the kitchen to find both Maw Maw and Paw Paw sitting at the table, studying the books.

One day I asked, politely, "Why are books always open on the table, and why do you leave them there?" Their response was quite impactful. They explained to me that they started their day with a Bible verse or passage. They followed that up with a devotion and maybe a book to reinforce the Scripture verse they were studying. They went on about their day, purposefully leaving the books open. They told me they would "feed" upon the verses all throughout the day. When they walked past the table, they stopped, reread a verse or passage, and "nibbled" on it. Maw Maw and Paw Paw thought upon the verse as they reread it while passing the table. This allowed what they were learning to settle in and take root in their day and their lives. They applied these Scripture verses to whatever they were doing or whatever they were going through.

My grandparents' approach of feeding upon the Word began to make so much sense to me. Jesus says in John 6:35 (ESV), "I am the bread of life; whoever comes to me shall not hunger, and whoever believes in me shall never thirst." Think about how Jesus often retreated to fill Himself in time of prayer with the Father. My grandparents "chewed" on the Word all throughout the day, allowing it to nourish their souls.

The lesson I learned that day also took a huge load off my shoulders, a mistaken belief I think many of us hold: We have to read a ton of the Bible each day. Not true. God's Word is powerful. If we only get the chance to read one verse a day, His Word can and will impact us. We only need to nibble on it all throughout the day and let it feed our Spirit. No matter how much we read, the point is that we must read and spend time with Him in prayer and in His Word, so we don't become malnourished. As Matthew 5:6 (ESV) says, "Blessed are those who hunger and thirst for righteousness, for they shall be satisfied."

After that day, when I learned about my grandparents' study habits, I walked into their kitchen and saw the beauty of all their books scattered about. I realized it was a beautiful display of their feast for the day. May we each take time today to open His Word and spend time with Him, our Bread of Life.

"Oh, taste and see that the Lord is good! Blessed is the man who takes refuge in him!" Psalm 34:8 (ESV)

"Man shall not live by bread alone, but by every word that comes from the mouth of God." Matthew 4:4 (ESV)

Prayer:

Thank You, Lord Jesus, for satisfying our hunger and thirst with the Word of God and Your presence. Help us take time each day to open Your Word and feed upon it. Let time with You be our fulfillment. In Jesus' name, amen.

Questions:

How did God speak to you as you read this story?

What is a favorite Bible verse or passage that you like to read and reflect upon?

Who in your life has encouraged you to grow closer to the Lord just by examining the way they live? Do you think they spend time in the Bible?

A Step Closer:

Here are some Scripture verses that talk about the power of God's Word: Isaiah 55:11, John 6:37, John 3:16, James 1:18, Hebrews 13:8, Hebrews 4:12, John 6:44, and Numbers 23:19.

Today is the perfect day to single out one verse or chapter in the Bible and feed upon it all throughout the day. See how it takes root in your heart and in your life and take note of the changes you eventually see. Here is a verse to start you off: John 4:14.

2

THE BRIDGE AND THE BENCH

Driving along Lake Pontchartrain on I-10 headed to New Orleans, there's an area to the left where all you see is miles and miles of water. At one particular spot, there are rows and rows of electric poles lined up perpendicular from the interstate headed north across the lake. This is our spot. Brett leans over and gives me a kiss as we say to each other, "I love you all the way around the world and back."

We have driven over that spot many times while dating, then married, married with babies, and now with kids who are old enough for us to share the story of this secret spot with them. Every time we drive over that spot from here on out, I know without a doubt that my husband will lean over and give me a smooch, and we will say those loving words to each other.

Back in Texas, while walking my dog, Roux, we come across a bench that sits on the edge of our neighborhood pond. Every time we approach the bench, my dog slows down, turns to look at me, and sits. She knows this is my spot—my spot with Jesus. There is a particular place on the bench where I sit and pray. I do this every day.

Admittedly, sometimes, if I am in a hurry or it's raining, I want to just rush past the spot and hurry back home. My dog does not like that. She is conditioned to stop and sit at that spot, and she calls me out when I don't. In a funny way, it's like she is holding me accountable.

It is in that spot on the bench where I sit in God's presence. I lay before Him my concerns, my fears, my heartache, my everything. It is also here that I just soak in the peace and joy God gives me, and I thank Him for it. Sometimes it is where I just sit and listen to all the sounds surrounding me. I listen to the water splashing in the pond, the ducks quacking and flying overhead, and the wind rustling the leaves in the trees. Most importantly, I listen for God's gentle voice in my soul. Colossians 3:16 (ESV) says, "Let the word of Christ dwell in you richly, teaching and admonishing one another in all wisdom, singing psalms and hymns and spiritual songs, with thankfulness in your hearts to God."

It is important for us to have a routine with God-time set aside for Him. Where is your special place with the Lord? Mine is sitting on a bench by the pond. My brother's is walking along the shores of the South Florida beaches. My daughter's is in a secret room underneath the stairwell. My friend's is in a prayer closet just off her bedroom. My niece's is on a grassy hill at a park near her home.

Jesus Himself retreated away from all the noise to pray and fill Himself with His Father's strength and peace. Mark 1:35 (ESV) says, "And rising very early in the morning, while it was still dark, he departed and went out to a desolate place, and there he prayed." Mark 6:46 (ESV) says, "And after he had taken leave of them, he went up on the mountain to pray." Luke 5:16 (CSB) says, "Yet he often withdrew to deserted places and prayed." Luke 6:12 (ESV) says, "In these days he went out to the mountain to pray; and all night he continued in prayer to God."

Although God hears your prayers wherever you are, it is special to create a place where you can sit in His presence daily and be surrounded by His peace. Let it be a place where you can often visit and wrap yourself in His love.

Just like I look forward to our special designated kissing spot on the bridge, I even more so look forward to my walks outside and my time spent on the bench. Why are these spots precious to me? It's because I know that when I drive away from that kissing spot, my heart is full, and I feel loved. And when I stand up from the bench after leaving whatever I was carrying at the feet of Jesus, I know I was heard and I know, once again, I am loved.

It says in the Bible (James 4:8) to draw near to God and He will draw near to you. How true this is! I know it to be true and real because I experience it. It also says in Psalm 23:3 (ESV) that "He restores my soul." That is what I know and feel every time I designate time spent alone with Jesus.

Whether it's a bridge or bench or wherever, find your special spot to bask in His presence. Let Him fill you as you empty out your heart to Him. Your loving Father is waiting to meet with you and let you know that He loves you bigger than the world.

Prayer:

Dear Lord Jesus, thank You for being patient with me while waiting to meet with me. Thank You for always having time to listen to me. Please forgive me for neglecting to spend time with You. Thank You for the peace that floods me when I take time to sit in Your presence. Help me talk to You all throughout the day no matter where I am and to consistently seek You with all my heart. In Your precious name, I pray, amen.

Questions:

What did God speak to your heart as you read this story?

Where is your designated prayer/quiet place with the Lord? If you don't yet have one, where could some possible places be?

Read the following verses and let them take root in your heart: Jeremiah 29:12–13 (NKJV): "Then you will call upon Me and go and pray to Me, and I will listen to you. And you will seek Me and find Me, when you search for Me with all your heart."

Psalm 16:11 (ESV): "You make known to me the path of life; in your presence there is fullness of joy; at your right hand are pleasures forevermore."

A Step Closer:

Here are some Scripture verses you can read to learn more about dwelling in God's presence: Psalm 26:8, Psalm 37:7, Psalm 85:8, 1 Kings 8:27, Psalm 132:5, Hebrews 4:16, and Revelation 21:3.

Here are some Scripture verses about being still: Psalm 46:10, Exodus 14:14, Mark 4:39, Psalm 37:7, Habakkuk 2:20, Psalm 131:2, and Psalm 23:2–3.

Roux sitting in her spot near my spot on the bench.

3

Front Yard Football to Sideline Cheer

Growing up, no matter where I was in my walk with the Lord, I always knew I should do two things: read my Bible and pray for my future husband. Looking back, I am so thankful I did just that.

I grew up pretty tough; some would call me a tomboy. You would often see me in the front yard playing any type of sport with my brother and all the neighborhood boys. At school, it was no different. If there was a game going on at recess, I was right there in the middle of all the boys.

At that time, my sister, brother, and I were heavily involved in competitive karate. Most every weekend, we traveled to karate tournaments to compete. There, once again, I was amongst mostly all boys. Very rarely would I compete against a girl since not many girls took karate back then. My siblings and I advanced pretty far in the karate world, often coming first in tournaments, winning championships, and even placing in the Junior Olympics.

My cousins were the dancers of the family and very good at it too. Two of my cousins became captains of the dance team at our local high school, which was very talented and just as revered as the cheer squad. When I reached high school, the cousin who was captain kept asking me to try out for the dance team. I was reluctant, had zero dancing skills, and only wanted to try out for volleyball and softball. It wasn't long until my cousin and several of my friends talked me into at least trying out for the dance team. My thoughts were, "It's a new experience, and it will be fun just to try out."

Each group of girls danced before the judge's panel twice. Each time, I forgot the routine but made up moves of my own and tried to play it off. Some girls beside me forgot the routine and ran off the stage crying. It was surely one of the most nerve-racking and humbling experiences I had faced at that time in my life. After embarrassing myself twice with my awful performances, we sat in the waiting room for the results to be announced. Again, I thought I was just there for my friends and was trying to comfort and encourage them in this new, fun experience.

The time came for the judges to announce the new team. I was sitting criss-crossed on the first of three rows of girls and remember wearing a blue and white leotard with blue biking shorts. Once the judges called out the new squad member's number, the chosen girls walked up to the front of the gym to join their new team members. When the judge kept calling out the number twenty-eight and no one stepped forward, a friend sitting next to me nudged me and said, "Cheri, that's you!" I panicked and thought for certain the judges got my number mixed up with someone else's.

After all the numbers were called out, still in shock, I made my way over to the judge's table and said, "Sir, I don't understand. I can't dance! Why did you choose me?" He replied, "Your toe touches and kicks were amazing, and even though you did not know the dance, you held your composure, continued to smile, and made up your own moves. We can teach you how to dance."

Remember, dancing was not something I wanted to do in place of other sports. I was not, in any way, shape, or form, graceful and I did not even know dance terminology. My poor cousin, being the captain, quickly had her work cut out for her with teaching me.

Dancing became a challenge, and I was determined to learn. By the third year of being on the high school dance team, I fell in love with it. All along, I prayed that I would get better at dancing, not let the team down, and for God to guide my steps in dance, as well as in life. Proverbs 20:24 (NIV) says, "A person's steps are directed by the Lord. How then can anyone understand their own way?"

After graduating high school, those of us dancers who went to LSU wanted to try out for the team there, called the "Golden Girls." My friends and I had a plan to take weekly dance lessons from a former Golden Girl in order to be ready for tryouts.

There was one catch with tryouts. We had to choreograph our own dance. When I heard that, I immediately called my friend, who was an NFL cheerleader and asked her to help me create a routine. She agreed to help me but asked why I wouldn't just try out for the NFL team and dance with her. I quickly declined and told her I was scared of driving in New Orleans and that dancing for the Saints would be too much time for me to spend away from Baton Rouge. However, she continued to encourage me and told me I could ride with her to and from practices as well as games and that practices were only twice a week.

Both the Golden Girl and the NFL Cheer team tryouts happened to be held on the same day in different cities, so I had to make up my mind about which team I would try out for. I went to bed searching through Scripture, hungry for God's guidance, praying for Him to open the right door and give me peace about my decision. Proverbs 3:5–6 (CSB) says, "Trust in the Lord with all your heart, and do not rely on your own understanding; in all your ways know him, and he will make your paths straight."

Surprisingly, God led me to the conclusion that I needed to try out for the Saints' dance team. Proverbs 16:9 (ESV) says, "The heart of man plans his way, but the Lord establishes his steps." The ultimate deciding factor boiled down to how the director treated the dancers. I asked my NFL cheerleader friend if the director was nice or strict with the girls. I knew the director of the Golden Girls was somewhat harsh. My friend reassured me that I was making the right decision by telling me the NFL cheer director was cool and often hung out with them. I wanted my dance/cheer experience to be fun, not stressful, so I decided to try out for the NFL New Orleans Saintsations cheer team.

After three days of grueling practices in New Orleans with rounds of cutbacks, to my surprise again, I made the team! Little did I know my making the team would eventually lead me to my husband. Brett was an NFL football player, playing receiver for the New Orleans Saints. All along, God was guiding Brett's steps as well. The journey that led him to me was equally, if not more, improbable. But that's his story to tell.

I now see clearly how God guided me down unforeseen paths that eventually led me to my soulmate. It was not me who chose to become a dancer. It was not me who had a dream to become an NFL cheerleader. My plans for my life looked completely different, so I can take no credit for what God did for me.

So many people had a hand in my making the high school dance team and eventually opening the door to my NFL experience. But above all, I praise God for His plan in leading this small town girl (once tomboy) into new territories and carving out the path for my future. As 1 Corinthians 2:9 (ESV) says, "But as it is written, 'What no eye has seen, nor ear heard, nor the heart of man imagined, what God has prepared for those who love him.'"

I am living proof that God answers prayers. By reading and trusting in His Word and praying for my future husband, He has indeed blessed me with a life and husband far better than I could have ever dreamed.

Prayer:

Dear Lord, when our lives seem chaotic and anxiety fills us regarding our future, please help us place our unknown in Your hands and trust that You will lead us down the best path. Help us read the Bible daily and pray for what lies ahead. We leave it all in Your hands and praise You for the many blessings You bestow upon us. In Jesus' name, we pray, amen.

Questions:

What memory came up for you as you read this story?

How have you seen God lead you away from the path you were walking and onto a new, better path?

"You make known to me the path of life; you will fill me with joy in your presence, with eternal pleasures at your right hand" Psalm 16:11 (NIV). What jumps out to you in this verse and why?

A Step Closer:

Here are some Scripture verses regarding God creating a path for you: Proverbs 19:21 and Matthew 6:25–34.

Here are some Scripture verses about trusting God's plan for your life: Romans 8:28, Proverbs 19:21, Psalm 32:8, Isaiah 40:31, Psalm 28:7, and Psalm 9:9.

Young Cheri fighting a boy
in a karate tournament.

Cheri — Friday night high
school football game

FRONT YARD FOOTBALL TO SIDELINE CHEER

Cheri — NFL cheerleader
(New Orleans Saintsation)

Brett — NFL football player
(New Orleans Saints)

4

LOSING MY DADDY

So often, I curled up in my daddy's lap with my head on his chest, playing with his Saint Christopher necklace in one hand while the other hand rubbed all the hair on his arm in the same direction. Looking at the scars on his hands and the one on his face, I would ask him to retell me the stories of how he got them. The ones on his hands came from hot tar splashing up from a bucket he was carrying while roofing. The spider web-looking scar next to his hazel eyes came from a brown recluse bite when he was just twenty-one years old.

Another story I asked him to tell was the one of him wearing a burlap outfit to school that his mother made him from potato sacks. They were very poor, and they did what needed to be done in order to make it in life. This propelled him to consistently work hard in hopes of one day earning enough money for regular clothes.

The truth is, I really didn't care what he was talking about, just as long as I was in his arms, listening to his voice. Needless to say, I adored my daddy. He was my hero. When he talked, I listened. I wanted nothing more than to spend time with him and please him.

It was the summer before my sixth grade year when my daddy first got sick. During that time with my family in the waiting room of the local hospital, my aunt told me about a young girl who was battling the same type of cancer my dad had, leukemia. My aunt explained that this girl would be coming to my school sometime in the fall after she completed her treatments at St. Jude and encouraged me to be on the lookout for her.

Sure enough, about a month into school, as I was sitting in my fourth-period science class, in walked this girl. The teacher stopped the lesson and said aloud, "Class, I would like for y'all to help me welcome our new student, Katie Kane."

I eagerly watched as Katie walked across the front of the room towards the center table and sat down directly in front of me. I quietly tore off a piece of notebook paper and wrote something like this: "Hi Katie! My name is Cheri Jackson. I'm happy to have you in class. My daddy has the same kind of cancer you do, so if you ever need a friend to talk to, I'm here." Thankfully, Katie and I hit it off and from that moment on, we were inseparable.

While most middle school girls were busy gossiping, scoping out boys, or finding the latest fashion (completely normal), Katie and I were battling life together. She was undergoing chemotherapy and fighting daily, just as my daddy was. We understood each other. In the chaos of our daily life struggles, Katie was like "home" to me. Yes, we still talked about boy bands and found similar interests in music and did normal tween stuff, but we had another layer of life that we were dealing with. And that bonded our friendship tightly together in a unique way.

Two years later, as I was sitting in my second period math class, a voice from the front office came over the intercom saying, "Please allow Cheri Jackson to check out now." I looked in the doorway and saw Katie, who had come to walk me to the front office. Because Katie could not participate in physical education, she was an office aide. I feared why I was being checked out as I slowly grabbed my book sack and walked out of the classroom into the dark hallway. I asked Katie, "Why am I being checked out of school?" She calmly told me she didn't know. We quietly walked to the office together. I didn't know what news awaited me, but I remember being so thankful for God providing me with my sweet friend to lead me down that hallway.

When I walked into the office and saw my mom there, I asked, "Why am I being checked out? What happened?" Mom gently wrapped her arms around me and guided me out of the office, saying, "Let's go outside." She walked me out to her car, but before we got in, she said, "Your daddy passed away this morning." I collapsed to the ground screaming, "Noooooo!" My mom just held me and tried to comfort me the best she could. She drove me to my Maw Maw's house, where the rest of the family was gathered to comfort each other.

My whole heart was ripped out right then and there when I lost my daddy. How could this be? What was I supposed to do now? I felt confused, broken and utterly empty.

Throughout the years, by reading the Bible, I found its words impactful and full of truth. I held on to every word that brought hope and life and peace into my broken world. At a ripe, young age, I learned to look to Christ as my Father, for nothing or no one else could fill that absence in my heart and my life.

God had to teach me that He is my Father, who will *never leave me*. He taught me how to trust in Him by leaning on His every Word. He beckoned me to come to know Him as we all are supposed to, as our loving Father. The Bible, in Mark 14:36, Romans 8:15, and Galatians 4:6 (NIV), refers to God as "Abba, Father." That is a loving way to call him "Daddy."

Thirty-something years later, as I was enjoying a peaceful day on the golf course with my husband, God pressed some words upon my heart. I did not tell them to my husband, but instead wrote the phrase on a piece of paper. I held onto it as I pondered the words the entire afternoon and let them sink into my soul. While being outside in the midst of God's raw beauty, I felt such an overwhelming amount of God's love flooding my entire being as I came to realize the heartache I endured so many years ago had a purpose.

All the years I allowed God's Word and Spirit to fill the emptiness and void I had by not having my earthly father with me, God was pouring His strength and wisdom in me. Just like a vase that was broken and put back together, God filled my crevices with Him and made me stronger and sturdier than I ever could have or would have been. Jesus is my Redeemer and made me whole and complete again.

It suddenly made so much sense to me ... the truth in what God was bringing to light for me to understand the phrase He pressed upon my heart.

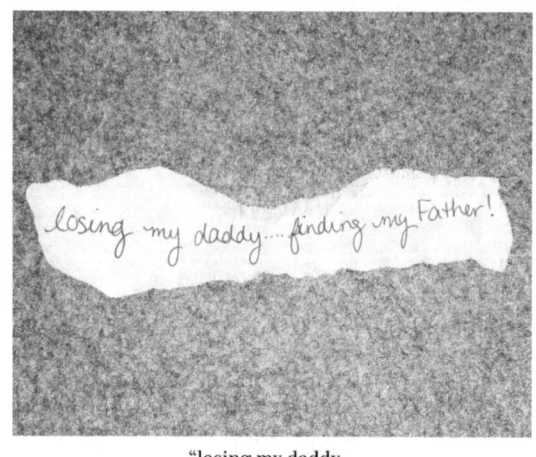

"losing my daddy...
finding my Father!"

You see, *in losing my daddy, I found my heavenly Father* in Jesus Christ.

Prayer:

Thank You, Lord, for giving us exactly what we need when we need it. Thank You for providing friends and family to help navigate the unforeseen bumps in the road. I praise You for being our loving Father and helping us better understand confusing moments in life. Thank You for redeeming what is broken in our lives and making it new and full again. In Your heavenly name, we pray, amen.

Questions:

What did God reveal to you as you read this story?

In what ways have you learned to let Jesus be your Father? Do you feel His love?

Looking closely at your life, do you see how God has provided friends in specific moments for you?

Read Philippians 4:19 (NIV): "And my God will meet all your needs according to the riches of his glory in Christ Jesus." How is this true in your own life?

A Step Closer:

Do you ever feel like everyone leaves you? Search through the Bible and see what it says about God *never* leaving you or forgetting about you. Here are some Scripture verses to help kick off your search: Deuteronomy 31:8, Hebrews 13:5, and Isaiah 49:15–16.

Here are some Scripture verses regarding friendships: Proverbs 17:17, Proverbs 18:24, Proverbs 27:17, Proverbs 22:24–25, and Ecclesiastes 4:9–12.

Note about friendship:

Throughout our middle school years, Katie and I depended on each other. She was and always will be very special to me. Our friendship was given to us directly from the Lord, and for that we are grateful. God knew what I needed and maybe what Katie needed in a friend at that time, too, and He provided just that. Our life battles during our middle school years helped us appreciate life and grow a genuine love for people. Although my dad lost his battle with cancer, Katie overcame hers. She now has a full life with a wonderful husband and darling children. I encourage you to pray for solid friends for yourself and your children. God will provide.

Katie and Cheri (6th grade)

5

Forgiveness = Freedom

Shortly before my dad got sick, due to lack of communication, my mom and dad's marriage ended. However, they kept trying to make amends and get back together. Unfortunately, by the time my dad got sick, a deceitful woman, whom I will refer to as "Stacy," immersed herself into our lives by swooning him in his time of desperation, and they quickly got married. There were red flags all along the way, but I honestly think my dad was just too weak and tired to end the new marriage.

I will forever treasure the memory of my mom, my siblings, and I going to see my dad in the hospital. We walked in, and as my mom tightly hugged him, he started crying, saying, "When I get out of here, I want us to get our little family back together again." Sadly, he never made it out of the hospital, and therefore, he passed away while still being married to Stacy and not my sweet mama.

After my dad passed, the following months in my life seemed like a blur. Stacy abruptly changed the locks on the doors of our home, prohibiting us, his kids, from going inside as she stole all of my dad's belongings. Not only had our world been turned upside down by the loss of our dad, but now we didn't even have our home. Worst of all, we later learned she tried to hire someone to fatally harm one of us. Life as we knew it was no longer a reality but felt like a horrible nightmare.

Through legal action, Stacy eventually admitted in court to forging my daddy's will in hopes of taking everything from us. She never returned all of his belongings and ultimately left us with nothing of his at all. I was robbed of the chance to ever hold one of my daddy's shirts to my face, smell his smell one last time, or even look upon his favorite worn-out cowboy boots or anything else that would have brought comfort to me in those lonesome moments.

Since we sometimes lived with our dad before he passed, my brother and I permanently moved in with our precious mama. She consistently turned to God for help in navigating this new route in life we all were forced to take, and by doing so, she unknowingly showed us how to move forward with strength from the Lord.

One day, not long after, as I was home alone, still thirteen years old, I felt God prompting me to do something unthinkable. I picked up the phone and called Stacy. I said, "I know what you've done, God knows what you've done, and now Daddy knows what you've done. I forgive you." And I quickly hung up the phone.

I forgave her.

Since that very moment, I have not held any anger, bitterness, or yuck in my heart toward her. God graciously taught me at a young age how to truly forgive and how, in *forgiveness, there is freedom*. God used my sweet mama to show my siblings and me this truth by exemplifying forgiveness over and over again throughout our lives. Psalm 86:5 (NIV) says, "You, Lord, are forgiving and good, abounding in love to all who call to you."

What I went through in losing my daddy was painful, but I have come to see clearly that God has never left my side. Not ever. He has filled and continues to fill my every void in such beautiful ways when I ask Him to. I realize my life could have been entirely different had I not learned to trust the Lord in the midst of my heartache. Psalm 32:8 (ESV) says, "I will instruct you and teach you in the way you should go; I will counsel you with my eye upon you."

As much as I wish my daddy were sitting in his chair again and for me to be wrapped up in his loving arms, listening to his calm voice … as much as I wish my daddy could take my husband and my girls fishing or for him to see what terrific young ladies Brett and I have been blessed with, I do not for one-second wish my daddy away from the Lord's presence. I trust that God's plan is perfect; therefore, I do not question it. I am who I am today because of that road, I had to take.

Everything I went through during that journey has left me with a deep appreciation for family, friendship, and life itself. I now make sure every person I am blessed to be surrounded with is loved to the fullest, and nothing is left unsaid between us. Romans 12:10 (ESV) says, "Love one another with brotherly affection. Outdo one another in showing honor."

What I am most thankful for is Jesus teaching me through all of this that through Him, there is abounding *freedom in forgiveness*.

Prayer:

Dear Lord, thank You for never abandoning us in times of loss. Your presence and love fill our cracks and emptiness. May we each learn to know You as our loving Father who never leaves us. No matter what road we have to take to learn that truth, may we come to know You as our ever-present Father and Lord of our lives. In Your precious name, we pray, amen.

Questions:

What thoughts or emotions rose up as you read this story?

In what ways have you found freedom in forgiveness?

Psalm 68:5 (CSB) says, "God in his holy dwelling is a father to the fatherless and a champion of widows." How does this verse bring comfort to you?

A Step Closer:

Here are some Scripture verses related to forgiveness: 1 John 1:9, Matthew 6:14–15, Colossians 3:13, Ephesians 4:32, Luke 17:3–4, and Mark 11:25.

Here are some Scripture verses about freedom: Galatians 5:1, 13–14, 22; 2 Corinthians 3:17; John 8:36; 1 Corinthians 6:12; Ephesians 3:12; Psalm 118:5; and Psalm 119:45.

My daddy and me
(3 years old)

6

Mud

One sunny Saturday afternoon, I was in my living room playing Legos when I heard a loud thump against my window. I ran to see what it was and found a huge mud ball splattered against the window pane, slowly dripping down. I looked past the muck and saw him—Milton Blake—peddling fast away from my yard on his bike, looking back and laughing.

I thought to myself, "Alright, that's okay. I will make him think I forgot about it, and in a few days, I'll get my revenge." I was already mad at Milton because the last time I went to play at his house, I saw my silver Mickey Mouse Pluto spoon he stole from me sitting on his desk. So, now I had two notches in my belt I was holding against him.

By Wednesday, I was ready. I hopped on my bike and slowly rode past his house. He was alone outside playing, and I said all nicely, "Hey Milton! Whatcha doing?" He, thinking I was oblivious to his prior offenses, was eager to play. He said, "Hey, wanna play?" I quickly turned my bike around, hopped off, and tackled him. I roughed him up pretty well by getting a few licks in. All the while, I was telling him how I knew about the Pluto spoon he stole and the mud pie he disrespectfully threw at my family's window. Then, I got on my bike and rode on.

I am not in any way, shape, or form condoning this behavior, which I chose to display at eight years old. However, growing up in the 80s looked a whole lot different than it does now. We, as kids, dealt with most situations by taking things into our own hands, not involving adults. However, my parents knew about the rivalry Milton and I had with each other.

So, at night, when we said our prayers, the hardest thing for me to do was what my parents had instilled in me—forgiveness and love. We Jackson kids often heard from our parents, "God called us to love everyone and not hate anyone." Matthew 5:43–44 (CSB) says, "You have heard that it was said, Love your neighbor and hate your enemy. But I tell you, love your enemies and pray for those who persecute you." I remember that each night for a few years, I said my prayers, and at the very end, I would say, "And I love everyone ... even Milton Blake."

At that young age, as hard as it was for me, I checked my heart to make sure I was not harboring any hate against my neighbor. Years later, in high school, I apologized to Milton for beating him up and giving him a black eye. He laughed about it, said he forgave me, and all was well.

Young or old, we all have our "enemies" in life. I am grateful for my parents teaching us to forgive and to truly love at such a young age. And I recall how hard it was to utter the words "even Milton Blake" at the end of my prayers, but I made sure I meant it before saying it. I still have to do this at my age. I have to give the flame of anger that tries to take root in my heart to God and ask Him to replace it with His love for that person, especially for the ones in life who try to bully me or my kids. The Bible says in Matthew 6:15 (NIV), "If you do not forgive others their sins, your Father will not forgive your sins." God will not hear our prayers when we have unforgiveness in our hearts (Isaiah 59:1–2).

Proverbs 11:27 (CSB) says, "The one who searches for what is good seeks favor, but if someone looks for trouble, it will come to him." This verse makes me think of looking at someone, enemy or friend, and not looking for the dirt on them, but searching for the jewel inside of them, just like Jesus does with us. The vertical part of the cross (loving God) is easy. It's the horizontal part that's hard. The part that has you reach out your arms wide to love others, just as Christ loves and forgives us. That's the part we battle with. May we remember how Jesus always displays this love for us, and if we expect Him to continue to wrap love and forgiveness around us, we must try to do the same to others—even Milton Blake.

"Surely the arm of the Lord is not too short to save, nor his ear too dull to hear. But your iniquities have separated you from your God; your sins have hidden his face from you, so that he will not hear." Isaiah 59:1–2 (NIV)

Prayer:

Dear Lord, thank You for using any means necessary to teach us how to love and forgive just as Jesus does. Let us remember that we, too, need much forgiveness. Please help us to check our hearts daily to make certain we are not harboring any hate or unforgiveness. And when we do find the yuck in our hearts, may we give it all to You and ask You to replace it with Your love. In Jesus' name, amen.

Questions:

What came up for you as you read this story?

Take a minute to think about who you may not be forgiving or who you have a hard time dealing with. Ask God to help you see them the way He does and to take your heart and rid it of any unforgiveness towards this person you are thinking of.

What times in your life have you forgiven others and felt freedom from doing so?

A Step Closer:

Here are some Scripture verses related to loving others: John 13:34–35, 1 John 4:7–8, Luke 6:31, 1 Corinthians 13, 1 Peter 4:8, Colossians 3:14, and 1 John 4:20.

Here are some Scripture verses that talk about praying for others: James 5:16, 1 Timothy 2:1–2, and Matthew 5:44.

Mickey Mouse "Pluto" spoon

7

SAVE ME, JESUS!

BIKE RIDING WAS ONE of our favorite daily activities when the girls were young. Late into the day, we all went riding as a family. However, if time permitted, I would sometimes take Cora and Olivia earlier, as well.

One morning, Cora was itching to go bike riding, because she was gaining confidence riding with her new training wheels. I told her that as soon as we finished our breakfast and did a few house chores, we could set out for an early bike ride. I pulled Olivia in the big red wagon and walked the dog while trying to closely follow Cora as she zoomed enthusiastically ahead of us.

We enjoyed the lovely day outside, doing what we loved to do, but I noticed Cora began to get a little reckless on her bike. She started going faster and faster and swerving sharply left, then sharply right. I called out to her, warning her that if she kept doing that, she was going to fall. She heard me but was so into her thrilling adventure that she chose to ignore me. Again I said, "Cora, you had better slow down or you are going to fall."

Sure enough, not long after that, Cora turned her wheel sharply to the left and took a tumble off her bike onto the road. It was not a bad fall whatsoever, and I saw that no damage was done to her little body. However, what she said as she was falling to the ground caused me to giggle uncontrollably. She loudly screamed out, "Save me, Jesus!"

I ran to her, trying to not giggle, but said, "Cora, you are okay, angel. God allowed for you to have a safe fall. But did you just yell out, "Save me, Jesus?" She said, "Yes, ma'am." I responded, "Cora, thank God you are okay, but I am tickled that you knew in that moment of fear to call out to Jesus to help you. I'm so proud of you!"

As I helped her dust her little legs off and get back on her bike, I talked to her about how important it is to listen to my warning and to be careful. She agreed, and we both thanked God that He helped her in her time of need. The Bible says in Psalm 142:1 (CSB), "I cry aloud to the Lord; I plead aloud to the Lord for mercy." Psalm 50:15 (CSB) says, "Call on me in a day of trouble; I will rescue you, and you will honor me."

This story has stuck with me all these years because, at five years old, a brave little girl knew in the moment of uncertainty and fear that she could call upon the Lord for help. I often think about that sweet little voice calling out for help, and how I literally saw God allow a soft landing for her.

In the Bible, Romans 10:13 (KJV) says, "For whosoever shall call upon the name of the Lord shall be saved." Psalm 91:15 (KJV) says, "He shall call upon me, and I will answer him: I will be with him in trouble; I will deliver him."

May we each have the faith of that sweet little child of God and know that, without a doubt, we can call on Him no matter when or where, and He will help us. Help may not come in the form we want, but God will deliver. Let our own trust be just as solid in Him, and may we never be ashamed to call upon the One who promises to help.

We sometimes try to go ahead of God's plan on our own, ignoring His call. To be honest, all the times in my life when I have gone ahead of God, it did not turn out too well for me or anyone involved. I am learning to slow down, seek His will, and move forward as I ask Him to guide my steps. Just remember, no matter how far we have veered off God's path for us, He is only a prayer away.

Prayer:

Thank You, Lord Jesus, for being our very present help in times of trouble. Thank You for always being so present in our lives that you are able to hear and help us. May we trust that as a loving Father, you are ready and willing to rescue us. In Your precious name we pray, amen.

Questions:

What came up for you as you read this story?

When have you noticed God rescuing or delivering you?

Can you name moments when you ignored warning signs the Holy Spirit was sending you? How did that turn out?

Take notice of how God gently guides and rescues you in the upcoming days. Do you realize He is always protecting you (sometimes in small detail, sometimes in great detail), regardless of you being aware of it or not?

A Step Closer:

Read Psalm 77:1–20 and see how David is crying out to the Lord for help.

Read Mark 10:46–52 and see how this blind man cries out to Jesus.

Olivia, Cora, Shilah, Priscilla (in stroller), my Mama. (Gulf Breeze, Florida)

8

HANDS

It was a Sunday morning. The sermon had just ended, and the congregation was standing, singing praise and worship music before the end of the service. Then, she spoke with boldness. An elderly lady near the middle section of the church had her hands lifted and eyes closed. "Come to Me. I see you. The wall between Me and you was not put there by Me. It was placed there by you thinking you are not worthy of My love. You are. I am here waiting for you to break down that wall and walk into My presence. You have already been forgiven. With Me in your heart, you are worthy. Do not let that wall keep you separated from Me. Trust Me and break through that wall. Do not let a second more go by. I am here. I love you." Then she looked around at the rest of us and said, "I do not know who that was meant for, but the Lord wanted me to say that to someone here."

Being a member of this church for almost a decade, I had never heard that lady speak out loud amongst everyone like she did that morning. She was a sweet, quiet, darling little lady, whom I only referred to as "the lady with the pretty hands." To this day, I still do not know her name. I saw her every Sunday morning and watched her reach upward in praise as she sang to her Savior. And I would just watch her hands and think how beautiful they were. I believe it wasn't just because her hands were pretty, but there was something that struck my attention in her pure love for the Lord and in her gentle worship.

After she spoke out in church, it was quiet for just a moment, then everyone continued to worship in song. I was frozen and shocked. The Lord Himself had just had this sweet lady speak His words directly to me. After crying and crying, I gathered myself, walked over to her, and told her, "Thank you for being obedient and speaking what God placed on your heart. That message was meant for me." She immediately wrapped her arms around me and hugged me. We spoke for just a moment and then each went on our way.

What if the sweet lady had not been obedient to the Lord's calling that morning? What if I hadn't gone to church? What if I hadn't been paying attention? Well, I am thankful that just as the Lord used her obedient little heart that morning, He also spoke to me in a way He knew I would clearly receive His message.

God is that good! He is that personal. I was blown away that He knew exactly what I was feeling and knew what to say to me. I loved going to church and believed everything I heard, but I always felt like the forgiven life and life lived for Jesus was for "the good people." I did not consider myself to be good enough. He knew how I felt and knew the wall in my mind was blocking my heart from welcoming Him.

The Bible says in Ephesians 2:14 (ESV), "For he himself is our peace, who has made us both one and has broken down in his flesh the dividing wall of hostility." The devil wants division. He wants us to feel not good enough and to keep a wall up that separates us from realizing we are meant to be with Christ. The Bible says in John 10:10 (ESV), "The thief comes only to steal and kill and destroy. I came that they may have life and have it abundantly."

It was because of one lady's obedience to the Lord and because God continued to pursue me, that I accepted Him as my Lord and my Friend that day in church. I had accepted Him as my Savior at the age of ten, which was about ten years before this moment described here, but I wasn't living in the truth and the fullness of Christ, because I was believing the devil's lies about me.

If you are feeling distant from Him, I urge you to tear down the wall! It is not meant to be there. You have access and are welcome in Jesus's presence. He wants you there, and He has not forgotten about you. 1 Timothy 2:3–4 says, "This is good, and it pleases God our Savior, who wants everyone to be saved and to come to the knowledge of the truth." Maybe God is calling you to reach your hands out to someone who is feeling divided and not worthy. Whatever it may be, trust that the Lord is reaching out His pierced hands to you. And those are the most beautiful hands in all creation.

"Today, if you hear his voice, do not harden your hearts." Hebrews 4:7 (ESV)

Prayer:

Dear Lord Jesus, thank You for knowing what our struggles are and for knowing exactly how to reach us. Please, Lord, let us hear Your voice and never harden our hearts. Please break down any barriers in our lives that are keeping us from surrendering to You. Let us believe that You lovingly accept us "as is" and that there is nothing we have done to make You unattainable. You are always right here reaching out with Your loving hands to forgive us and welcome us in Your embrace. May we let You love us and allow You into our lives. Thank You, heavenly Father. It's in Jesus' name we pray, amen.

Questions:

What thoughts or emotions rose as you read this story?

Do you think you are not "good enough" to have a relationship with Christ? Search the Bible for Scripture verses that prove you wrong. You are never too far gone. He forgives and does not hold your past sins against you when you ask Him into your heart and ask for forgiveness.

What in your life is keeping you from surrendering to Jesus? Ask Him to crush down the barrier that was not placed there by Him.

Who in your life has been a witness to you and introduced you to Jesus? Take a moment and thank God for that person and lift them up in prayer.

A Step Closer:

Read Luke 23:44–47 and Matthew 27:51 to see how the veil was torn, symbolizing the direct contact we have with God Himself through Christ dying on the cross.

Read John 14:3 and John 14:15–23 to learn how God desires to have a relationship with us.

9

HEARING

So many times, we went to my Maw Maw and Paw Paw's house and noticed that Paw Paw, once again, had lost his hearing aids. I never understood how he could lose them so much and how we could never find them. Until one day …

I walked into the living room where Paw Paw was snuggled up in his recliner, watching TV very loudly. I said, "Paw, I'm going to find your hearing aids right now." I must have looked for a good twenty minutes, not finding them anywhere, while Paw Paw sat and watched TV, unfazed by my searching efforts. Then, I looked closely in between the magazines next to his recliner and said, "Paw! Look! I found them!" He immediately tapped my hand to get my attention and put his pointer finger up to his mouth, signaling "hush" to me. I dropped my jaw when I realized he was hiding them so he couldn't hear Maw Maw. I looked up at him, and he had a huge smile on his face as if saying, "This is our secret."

How hilarious! I laughed and laughed in amusement at my funny Paw Paw. Now, you have to understand, my Paw Paw loved my Maw Maw deeply, but in his defense, she was *so loud*! Her laugh, her voice, all of it. She was just a very loud human being. Fun-loving, but loud. So, Paw Paw chose when he wanted to "hear" her and when he didn't.

This makes me think of how many times we do this to Jesus in our lives. How often do we choose to ignore His voice? Do we hear Him and selfishly decide to follow our own path and walk away from Him? Truthfully, we all have done this and still do this to our loving Father's gentle call. We, like my Paw Paw, did to my

Maw Maw, make a conscious decision to turn down His voice in our lives and do our own thing.

In the Bible, Jonah did this same thing to God, and it didn't turn out too well for him. God asked Jonah to go to the sinful city of Nineveh and tell them they were doing wrong and to change their ways. Jonah chose not to because he didn't care for the Ninevites and didn't think they deserved God's grace. Jonah was not only hurting himself by choosing to ignore God, but he was prohibiting an entire city of people from hearing God's message. After spending three days in the belly of a whale, Jonah decided to listen to God and send the Ninevites His message. The people of Nineveh repented and changed their lives around because of one man's decision to finally obey God's calling.

Matthew 13:15 (ESV) says, "For this people's heart has grown dull, and with their ears they can barely hear, and their eyes they have closed, lest they should see with their eyes and hear with their ears and understand with their heart and turn, and I would heal them." The more you choose not to respond to God's voice, the harder it will be to hear Him, and eventually, you will not hear Him at all. This is a dangerous place to be, considering your heart will be hardened, and it will become difficult for you to differentiate between right and wrong, causing confusion in your life.

On the other hand, the more you listen to God's voice, the easier it will be for you to recognize it, allowing your heart to become sensitive to His calling. Romans 10:17 (ESV) says, "So faith comes from hearing, and hearing through the word of Christ." This not only helps you, but those around you. You will be a usable vessel for God to work in and through.

Psalm 85:8 (ESV) says, "Let me hear what God the Lord will speak, for he will speak peace to his people." And in John 10:27 (ESV), Jesus says, "My sheep hear my voice, and I know them, and they follow me."

God bless my sweet Paw Paw for what I caught him doing all those years ago, but one thing is for certain: my Paw Paw definitely listened to our heavenly Father's voice. His life clearly showed it. He shared Jesus with anyone who would listen, and he did it in such a gentle, loving way.

In my Paw Paw's last days, he became forgetful and couldn't remember much of anything. However, when we started singing old hymns, he would sing along with us and knew every single word. Maybe God's Word and praise that He is due is so powerful that no matter what else clutters our minds throughout the years, the Truth remains. Isaiah 40:8 (ESV) says, "The grass withers, the flower fades, but the word of our God will stand forever." Because of this, may each of us choose daily to acutely listen for our Father's voice and obediently walk toward it.

Not long before my Paw Paw made his entrance to heaven, God blessed me with this departing gift. I was sitting next to my Paw Paw, and he patted my hair ever so gently. I looked over at him and noticed him smiling so sweetly at me, and I asked, "Paw Paw, do you know who I am?" He said, "Of course I do. You're Cheri. I love you."

That was my last moment with my Paw Paw before he *heard* Jesus calling his name on this side of heaven one last time. May we learn to tune out all the other noises in life and tune into the only voice that matters—Jesus' voice—and choose to follow Him. It's the sound that will lead us to eternity with Him.

"When he calls to me, I will answer him." Psalm 91:15 (ESV)

Prayer:

Dear Heavenly Father, please help us not plug our ears in laziness or self-centeredness. May we hear You calling us and turn to You in loving obedience so You can teach us, guide us, and use us all for Your glory. We humbly ask this of You, in Jesus' name, amen.

Questions:

What did God speak to your heart as you read this story?

How do you find yourself tuning out God's voice in your life?

In what ways do you feel God calling you right now?

A Step Closer:

Here are some Scripture verses pertaining to listening to God's calling: Isaiah 28:23, Psalm 116:2, Proverbs 8:33, John 8:47, and Luke 11:28.

Here is a Scripture verse that refers to God's enduring love: 1 Peter 1:25.

Paw Paw and his dog Mellie

10

Put It Down

I WAS IN THE middle of painting my spare room one evening while pouring out my troubles to God in prayer when I felt God say, "Put it down. And go put the sign in the yard." I paused for a moment, then shook my head, thinking I was making it all up, and began painting again. Stretching the paint stick out to continue the job at hand, I felt it again. "Put the paint stick down and go put the sign in the front yard."

Placing the paint stick down, I walked into the kitchen and told my brother God was telling me to stop what I was doing and to go put the "for sale" sign in the yard. He responded, "Okay, but right now? It's raining outside." It was, in fact, raining, and it was 8:00 at night. You would think we could just wait until the morning to put the sign outside and continue painting for a few more hours. But that wouldn't have been obeying what God was telling me to do. So, we stopped painting and put the sign out in the front yard. I was exhausted and happy to just call it a night and get some rest.

The whole reason my girls and I were in Louisiana was to take care of my mom. She had just been diagnosed with cancer and underwent a major "exploratory" surgery. Brett had left for training camp in California with the Cowboys and would be gone for four weeks. My brother, sister, and I were each rotating turns taking care of Mom.

When we arrived in Louisiana, I found out that some of my daughters contracted hand, foot and mouth disease, so we weren't able to stay at my mom's house in fear of getting her sicker while she was trying to heal from surgery. We also couldn't stay with my in-laws because Brett's brother and wife had a sweet little newborn baby. While I was trying to find out where to stay, my former neighbor called and said our renters "just up and left" our house that we were renting out. They not only left without pay or warning, but they left our once beautiful home in shambles. As upset as I was, I figured it was at least a place the girls and I could stay while we were in town.

When I walked in to see the damage done to our home, I was shocked! Their dogs had ripped our courtyard and each wooden post to shreds. Dog feces were smeared all over the back porch, Sharpie marks covered our wooden cabinets and walls, the carpets had stains all over them, and the list goes on and on. It was mortifying to see our lovely home that held so many precious memories almost now unrecognizable.

At that moment, I felt so overwhelmed. Brett was gone, my mom was sick, my kids were sick, and now I had my hands full in having to clean up the absolute mess of the house in hopes of selling it. On top of all that, I could not even do what I came to Louisiana to do, which was to spend time with and take care of my sweet mom. Thankfully, precious family members and friends came to the rescue to help out with the kids and help clean up our house.

The next morning, after I sent my kids to a friend's house, cleaned up a bit, and changed clothes, I rushed out the door, so happy to finally get to see my Mom. I got about five minutes down the road when someone called me with interest in seeing my house that just went up for sale. I kept driving towards my mom's house while telling them they would have to wait because we had a lot of work to do on it before it would be ready to show. They insisted on seeing it *now*. I kept telling them no. They then said, "We are already walking around the outside looking in all the windows. It's okay if it's in bad shape. We understand."

I was so embarrassed that they had already walked around the back, smelling the dog mess and seeing my lovely home in such a wretched form. I slowly turned my truck around and agreed to come show them the inside. I kept feeling this would be such a waste of time because they were going to be disgusted by what they saw, and I honestly just wanted to go see my mom.

The entire time we walked the premises of the house, I apologized for the mess. I repeatedly told them what a gorgeous home this could be and that we had a ton of work to do on it. I mentioned that I was able to get an appointment the very next week to get the carpet in all the bedrooms replaced and that I should have all the walls painted by then.

The sweet couple was quiet and did not say much the entire time I was with them. Finally, we walked outside; they shook my hand, thanking me for coming back to show them around, and hopped in their truck. I stood there in the heat of the Louisiana summer, smelling dog dung, watching what would've been a potential buyer back out of my driveway. I felt defeated.

Then, as I was still standing there, I saw them stop, put their truck in drive, and head back up toward my house. The couple jumped out of the truck and said, "Ma'am, we have been praying for a house to become available in this neighborhood for about a year now. We ride through here every day looking for a for sale sign to pop up. In fact, we were here yesterday at 4:30 in the afternoon, and you did not have that for sale sign outside. When we drove by this morning, we knew this was our home. We want to buy your house for the price you are asking and take it 'as is.' And you can cancel the carpet appointment. My boy has allergies, and we would've just ripped it out anyway."

With tears in my eyes, I shared with them about God telling me to stop painting and put the sign outside in the yard. We discussed how we were praying on both sides of this story and how God swept in and blessed us both with what we needed.

After the agreement was signed and they drove away, I hit my knees, thanking God! Up until that moment, I was feeling like Job in the Bible. I felt like everything around me was crumbling, and there was no way I could do all I needed to do. God knew my heart and knew that all I wanted to do was take care of my mom. The love I felt from God overwhelmed me. As great and majestic as He is, He is still a loving Father who wants to help His struggling children. He is faithful!

I felt this verse come alive: "Then Jesus said, Come to me, all of you who are weary and carry heavy burdens, and I will give you rest" Matthew 11:28 (NLT).

And "Give all your worries and cares to God, for he cares about you" 1 Peter 5:7 (NLT). Jesus Himself gently reached out and took the burden off my shoulders and lovingly reminded me that when I obey Him, and *put it all down* at His feet, all will be well.

Prayer:

Dear Lord, thank You for moments in life when we trust and obey You, You show us what You are capable of. Help us be aware of areas in our lives where we need to stop, put down all the worry, ask for Your help, and actually trust that You will help us in whatever way You see fit. Thank You for Your abundant grace and for loving us so much! In Jesus' name, amen.

Questions:

How did God speak to you as you read this story?

Do you feel overwhelmed and defeated like Job in the Bible? What areas in your life can you call out to the Lord for help and lay your burdens at His feet?

Is it hard for you to trust that God can rescue you? Read through the following verses and pray over them: Matthew 7:7, John 16:24, and Philippians 4:6–8.

Stop right now and take a moment to see where God may be asking you to relinquish control and give it to Him. Ask Him to show you clearly the next steps to take and then thank Him.

A Step Closer:

Here are some Scripture verses to reinforce our knowledge of God's abundant grace: 1 Timothy 1:14, 1 Corinthians 15:10, Ephesians 2:8, 1 Corinthians 1:3, Philippians 1:2, and 2 Corinthians 13:14.

Here are some Scripture verses pertaining to finding rest in God: Isaiah 40:31, Psalm 23:1-2, Psalm 46:1, 2 Corinthians 12:9, Exodus 33:14, and Galatians 6:9.10

11

Pink Barbie Slipper

Loading up my toddlers, Cora and Olivia, into the double stroller while being very pregnant with number three was no easy task. While buckling Cora in, I noticed she was holding her Barbie doll tightly in her hand. I told her not to bring it into the mall because, most likely, she was going to lose it. She begged me to let her hold onto it and swore she wouldn't let it go.

We went in and out of many stores until we had finished our shopping. Heading back out to my truck, I noticed the clouds were bringing in a storm, so I hurried to get the girls out of the stroller, settled them in their seats in the truck, and loaded the stroller in the back. Just as I stepped in and closed the door, the rain began coming down in buckets. We started the trek back to our New York home in the pouring rain. The journey was usually thirty minutes, but in bad weather, it took much longer.

As we pulled into the driveway, I unloaded each girl one at a time and ran them inside, while trying not to let them get soaked. Finally, we were all in, and Cora looked down at her Barbie still grasped in her hand and said, "Oh no, Mommy! Barbie's pink slipper is gone!" Seeing how worried she was, I knelt down beside her and said, "Let's pray about it. God knows where her slipper is, and we can ask Him to help us find it." We prayed earnestly and thanked God in advance for helping us find the lost shoe.

I'm not gonna lie, I was frustrated because I had asked her not to bring Barbie into the mall at all, knowing there was a good chance we were going to lose it. Also, it was still pouring down rain, and, needless to say, I was tired. Nevertheless,

I had the girls wait inside while I went back out in the downpour to search the stroller, the car seat, and the entire truck. As I was intently looking, I prayed for God to reveal where it was. After exploring every crevice of the truck, I still had no pink Barbie slipper.

Eventually, I stepped out of the truck, closed the door, and noticed something as I was about to walk away. There, on the step rail of the truck, sat the little pink Barbie slipper. I was shocked! You have to understand that my truck was an older model, and the guard rails did not retract when the door closed, meaning the rail was out in the open pouring rain the entire time. Even if the shoe had fallen out as I was unloading the girls, the rain was so heavy that it should have washed the shoe to the ground, where it would have floated away towards the drain.

In the dark of the night, through the pouring rain, I reached down, grabbed the pink shoe, and ran back to my girls, thanking God the whole way. I was trying to hold back my tears as I thought how precious it was of God to do this for that sweet three-year-old little girl. As I ran through the house door, I leaned over, opened my hand, and showed the girls the pink Barbie slipper. Cora gasped when she grabbed it out of my hand and happily put it back on Barbie's foot.

I went to bed that evening, thanking God for strengthening the faith of both toddlers and this one adult. He heard Cora's little heartfelt prayer and responded. That very night, God chose to help Cora's faith grow in a huge way from a very tiny little slipper. The Bible says all we need is the faith of a mustard seed. Matthew 17:20 (ESV) says, "For truly, I say to you, if you have faith like a grain of mustard seed, you will say to this mountain, 'Move from here to there,' and it will move, and nothing will be impossible for you." I held onto that little shoe for many years in hopes of reminding me that something so small and seemingly insignificant used by God can impact someone's faith in such a mighty way.

Do you know how many times throughout my girls' lives God has done things like that? So much so that anytime we lose an item, we look to each other and ask, "Have you prayed about it? God knows exactly where it is."

Many years later, on Cora's high school graduation day, I wrote her a letter reminding her of this story. I encouraged her to remember that if she ever feels lost when she goes off to college, God knows exactly where she is; all she has to do is reach out to Him in prayer. He will never let her lose her way, just like He proved to her so long ago on that rainy night in New York. Atop the letter I wrote to my daughter, I taped the very same tiny, pink Barbie slipper.

Prayer:

Dear Father God, thank You for Your wisdom and love You flood us with when we ask it of You. May we each remember that no matter what we need, You are our Provider, and all we need to do is come to You in prayer and trust You. No matter how insignificant we feel our needs are, You already know about them, and You are ready to help us and guide us. Thank You for being such a caring Father who is ever-present. In Jesus' name, amen.

Questions:

What did God reveal to you as you read this story?

Mark 11:24 (NIV) says, "Therefore I tell you, whatever you ask for in prayer, believe that you have received it, and it will be yours." In what ways do you believe this verse to be true?

Philippians 4:6–7 (ESV) says, "Do not be anxious about anything, but in everything by prayer and supplication with thanksgiving let your requests be made known to God." Take a moment now to do just as this verse says, and thankfully ask God anything and everything that you are anxious or concerned about. He is eagerly waiting to help you because He loves you.

A Step Closer:

Here are some Scripture verses highlighting God's infinite wisdom: 1 Corinthians 2:7, James 1:5, Luke 11:49–53, Proverbs 8:1–36, Proverbs 2:6, and Romans 11:33.

Here are some Scripture verses pertaining to going to God in prayer: Hebrews 11:6, 1 Chronicles 16:11, 1 Chronicles 28:9, Psalm 105:4, Matthew 7:7, Matthew 6:33, and Amos 5:4.

Pink Barbie slipper

12

SEEK

On a hot August evening, all six of us, Brett, Cora, Olivia, Shilah, Pippy, and I crouched down as we searched through the long, thick blades of grass. It was getting late in the day and the sun would be setting soon. We needed to hurry and find what we were looking for.

We were spending Brett's fiftieth birthday weekend at a ranch in West Texas and had enjoyed a fun-filled day of fishing, zip lining, and rock wall climbing. On the way back to our cabin, we stopped off in a nearby field to play a game of tetherball. After playing for a while, we started walking away when I realized something felt different on my finger. The diamond was missing from the ring my mom gave me; my daddy had given her that diamond for their wedding.

I could barely say what was wrong without crying, but once I got it out, we all immediately went back to the grassy area near the tetherball and started searching. Every person in our family knew what the diamond meant to me. My mom gave it to me when I graduated high school, and for at least a decade, I would not take it out of my jewelry box for fear of losing it. Then, one day, I realized it would mean nothing to my girls when I passed it on to them if they never saw me wearing it.

As my husband, my girls, and I searched between every two-inch blade of grass, we each silently prayed. My nervous prayer was something like this, "Dear Lord Jesus, oh dear Lord, please, please! You know exactly where this diamond is. Please, Jesus, please let one of us find it. Thank You!" Then, I decided to say to my family, "Whoever finds the diamond will be the one to get my ring when it's time for me to give it away." Somehow, right then, after I said that, I knew who was going to find it.

Regardless we continued looking, continued praying, and continued hoping. I looked around and saw some of the girls still searching, but they were losing hope and not searching as eagerly as they once were. Tears began to fill my eyes and I feared we would not find it.

Then, I heard the words, "I found it!" I looked up and saw Shilah smiling so big as she held the diamond up and placed it in my hand. I then let tears of happiness flow as we all hugged each other and rejoiced over finding the lost treasure. We were all emotional and couldn't stop thanking God for allowing us to find what we so desperately searched for.

Every now and then, when I glance at my ring, I think about the day we were so eager to find something so precious. And I think about the story in the Bible of the woman who lost her coin. It says in Luke 15:8–9 (NIV), "Suppose a woman has ten silver coins and loses one. Doesn't she light a lamp, sweep the house and search carefully until she finds it? And when she finds it, she calls her friends and neighbors together and says, 'Rejoice with me; I have found my lost coin.'" She did not halfheartedly look for her coin, but it says she "carefully" looked until she found it. Also, the verse found in Jeremiah 29:13 (NIV) says, "You will seek me and find me when you seek me with all your heart." It says *when* we seek with *all* of our heart, *then* we will find Him. If we are eager to know our precious Savior and search carefully for Him, we are promised to find Him.

Shilah never stopped searching. And because she never stopped, she found the diamond.

We were looking for a lost rock that summer day, and we found it and rejoiced. How joyous Jesus must be when we, who are lost, find Him, our precious Rock! The Bible describes Jesus in Psalm 18:2 (NIV): "The Lord is my rock, my fortress, and my deliverer; my God, my rock, in whom I take refuge, my shield and the horn of my salvation, my stronghold."

We are all lost without Christ, our Savior. We each feel a deep void and a constant yearning for something we know we need. Something that can only be filled with Christ. He is our source of joy, peace, calmness, security, purpose, forgiveness, and everything else good. Once we find Jesus and ask Him to come into our hearts and change us, then we begin to feel a sense of peace and belonging.

My sweet, precious daughter diligently searched for my daddy's diamond. And how very fitting for her to have found it, for she is named after my daddy. May each of us search for our Father with *all* of our hearts until we find Him. Then, we can rejoice and proudly carry Christ's name as His own children ... *Christ*ians.

Prayer:

Dear Lord Jesus, our Savior, our Rock, our Deliverer, thank You for being our stronghold in this ever-changing life we live. Thank You for allowing us to find You and know You when we truly seek you. May we find comfort in Your love for us. In Jesus' name we pray, amen.

Question:

What came up for you as you read this story?

How do you seek Jesus? I find Him through reading His Word and through prayer.

What do you think your benefit would be in finding Christ?

A Step Closer:

Here are some verses about seeking God: Matthew 6:33, Proverbs 8:17, Deuteronomy 4:29, 1 Chronicles 16:11, Hebrews 11:6, and 1 Chronicles 22:19.

Here are some verses about rejoicing in the Lord: Deuteronomy 12:7, Deuteronomy 16:11, Psalm 5:11, Psalm 32:11, Zephaniah 3:14, Zechariah 9:9, and Luke 10:20.

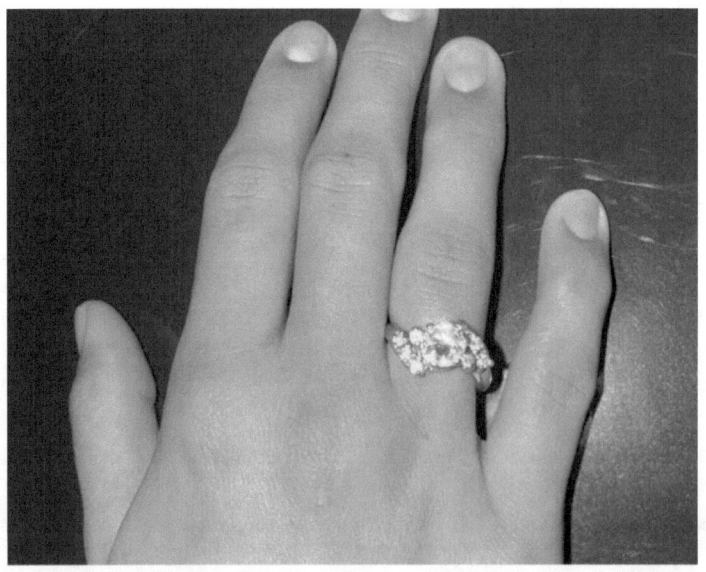

Shilah's wearing the ring that holds the diamond that daddy gave mom on their wedding day

13

Turn Around

Driving down Greenwell Springs Road, headed to my college class at LSU, I noticed an old, old man sitting in the median on a folding chair, holding a sign stating he was hungry. This was no new scene for me because I passed many homeless people here and there while driving the streets of downtown Baton Rouge. But this morning was different.

As I passed the elderly man with his long, gray, scraggly beard, I felt God nudge me. He impressed on my heart, "Turn around and feed him in My name." I said to myself, "I am late for my class. Surely it isn't God telling me to stop in this dangerous area, walk across the traffic lanes, and approach this strange man." Again, He pressed on my heart, "Turn around."

Reluctantly, I turned my little red car around and parked it in the 7-Eleven parking lot nearby. In the store, I purchased a turkey sandwich, an orange Gatorade, and a red bag of Doritos. I carefully walked across the lanes of traffic toward the gentleman, handed the food to him, and said, "Jesus loves you." He kindly thanked me, and I ran back to my car.

I quickly started my car and drove past the man still sitting in the chair. As I looked in my rearview mirror, I nearly wrecked—the man was no longer there! I turned my head around to see with my own eyes, and sure enough, the man, the sign, the chair ... all of it was gone! How could this be? I just saw him sitting there as I drove past, and now he and all of his belongings were gone. I whipped my car around to further check out the situation. Not only was he gone, but he was nowhere to be seen. I looked all over the nearby parking lots and streets, and there was no sign of him. You must understand that this man could barely move. He was so old and frail. There is no way on earth he could have quickly run off with all of his stuff without me being able to see him.

Still puzzled, I slowly drove back toward my class at LSU. After a few minutes of wondering what had just happened, the Bible verse in Hebrews 13:2 (CSB) came to mind. "Don't neglect to show hospitality, for by doing this some have welcomed angels as guests without knowing it."

A few years later, I found myself in a similar situation. In the heat of one Louisiana summer, while I was driving down Jefferson Highway, headed to my mom's office, I passed an elderly lady walking down the sidewalk near an apartment complex. The sight of this lady should not have caught my attention. But it did. God nudged me like He had done a few years before. "Turn around and help her."

I started questioning Him. "Ummmm, that lady seems to be just fine. She probably lives right there in one of those apartments. Why would I go bother her?" He put on my heart, "Turn around and go to her."

I reluctantly but obediently turned my car around. Getting back to her was no easy task. I had to go way down the road until there was a place for me to turn around and wait at a few lights before I could reach her. The whole time, I honestly thought, and kind of hoped, she would not still be there by the time I circled back. However, she was still there, walking along the sidewalk. I felt terrible for her because the temperature was in the upper 90s, and the still air was stifling hot. If nothing else, I needed to encourage her to go inside the apartment office to get out of the heat and into the fresh, cool air. Regardless, I pulled my little red car over, rolled down the passenger window, and asked her, "Ma'am, are you okay?"

Immediately, she stopped walking, and with a dazed look on her face, she said, "I … I don't know where I am." At that very moment, I knew God was right. He wanted me to help this confused lady. I jumped out, opened the door, and explained to her that I could help. I encouraged her to settle into my cool, air-conditioned car and drove her toward my mom's office nearby.

I kept asking her if she knew where she lived. She kept saying, "I don't know. I don't know." She was fumbling through her purse (which bizarrely only contained about fifty napkins), looking for her license. She was eventually able to tell me her first and last name, and with that, I brought her to my mom's office.

Once we gave the sweet lady cold water and sat her down to cool off, my mom introduced herself. Having dealt with her grandmother, who had suffered from Alzheimer's, my mom knew how to ask specific questions in order to trigger the forgetful lady's memory. Eventually, we found her address and were able to look up her phone number. My mom called the number and asked the voice on the other end of the phone if they had been looking for someone. The man responded, "We have been searching for my wife for four hours now. The police are here trying to help me."

After explaining to her husband what happened, I quickly walked the precious lady back to my car and took her back home. Her anxious husband was standing in the driveway, eagerly waiting for her. He happily greeted her with a huge hug and tears in his eyes. Taking in the beautiful scene for a few minutes and realizing all was well, I quietly left the couple with tears rolling down my face.

While driving away from their home, I asked myself, what if I had chosen to ignore God's calling that hot afternoon? Of course, God could have used someone else to help the lost lady, and I was not by any means her savior, but for me, what if I had kept driving past the lady and let God's voice get distant in my ears?

I believe God used these two instances to teach me how to listen for His voice, how to recognize it, and how to obey. John 10:27 (ESV) says, "My sheep hear my voice, and I know them, and they follow me." God is always speaking to us, like a loving Father does, trying to refine us, teach us, and help our faith grow, but how often are we listening? These moments where God nudged me have taught me to differentiate from His voice and all the other noise I hear and to understand and even appreciate how He beckons me.

Just like in the Bible, God called Samuel's name over and over and over before Samuel realized it was God calling him. It takes moments where we are still enough to listen for His voice and respond, "Okay, God. Here I am, Your servant. How can I obey today?" How many times in my life had He been calling my name, and I just didn't realize it was Him?

I drove away from that little lady's house, thinking of how God could have chosen to use anyone, but instead, He chose me. I am humbled and honored when He calls me to do His will.

When Samuel finally understood it was God calling, he eagerly waited for Him to call his name out again so he could answer. In 1 Samuel 3:10 (ESV) we read, "And the Lord came and stood, calling as at other times, 'Samuel! Samuel!' And Samuel said, 'Speak, for your servant hears.'" May we wake each day with the same eagerness and anticipation, waiting for God to nudge us, His special servants, to help someone today.

After all, it could be an angel we are helping …

Prayer:

Dear Heavenly Father, thank You for helping us to recognize Your voice. Help us clearly hear You above the rest of the noise surrounding us. Thank You for choosing us to do Your will here on earth and for allowing us to help others in Your name. It's in Your name we pray, amen.

Questions:

What did God reveal to you as you read this story?

What is God calling your name for? What has He called you to do recently? Are you actively listening for His voice?

How has God used you in the past to help others? Are you thankful He chose to use you?

A Step Closer:

Here are some Scripture verses related to obeying God: Deuteronomy 27:10, 1 John 5:3, Isaiah 1:19, Jeremiah 7:23, Luke 11:28, Deuteronomy 30:10, Ephesians 6:5, and Job 36:11.

Here are some Scripture verses about the importance of listening to God: Proverbs 5:1–23, Psalm 128:1–6, and Deuteronomy 28:1–68.

14

CROSSROADS

WHEN I WAS AN NFL cheerleader, often after games, we met up with friends and family across from the Superdome at a place called Hi Tops. One particular evening, I ordered a fruity drink, took one sip, set it down to turn around and say hello to a friend, turned back around, took another sip, and stepped away to go to the bathroom.

The next thing I experienced was the scariest moment in my life. I woke up in an unknown place. I was lying in a bed in a room I had never seen before. I looked around the room and didn't recognize anything. I looked on the dresser nearby, and atop the mirror, I saw a team cheer picture of me with a heart drawn on it! What in the world? Where was I?

Earlier in the evening at Hi Tops, across the room, I saw a guy from my hometown, Darron, who had been following me. Back home, everywhere I went, Darron would just appear. Friends of mine told me he was "chasing after me." He was not a good guy by any means and had a terrible reputation for using narcotics and doing bad things to girls. It terrified me whenever he'd suddenly show up, so as soon as I saw him, I would quickly leave.

One Sunday, when I was in the middle of cheering at a game, I saw Darron in the stands waving his arms and screaming my name. I felt shaken on the inside but tried to hold it together. A fellow cheerleader saw him and said, "Cheri, there's a guy up there yelling your name." I quickly told her to ignore him and that I did not want to make eye contact with him.

Back to my real-life nightmare. When I awoke in that strange room and started screaming, Darron popped up off the floor. I was in his apartment! Realizing this, I started screaming even louder. He tried to tell me that I was lucky he was at Hi Tops last night and that he was my hero. He said he "rescued me from someone who slipped drugs into my drink." I frantically kept screaming, "What did you do to me?" Suddenly, I stopped screaming when I realized I needed to hold my composure. For I was alone with the devil himself in this room and needed to get out. Eventually, I calmed myself down and made Darron take me to my car. When I got home, I ran to the shower, changed into some clean clothes, locked myself in my room, and sank into my bed crying.

I am not pretending to be a perfect angel, but you have to understand that I did not sleep around, and I had never tried drugs of any kind. So, I felt completely violated on every level. The worst part of it was that I had never been in a situation before where I wasn't in control of what was going on with me. I could not, no matter how hard I tried, make myself remember what happened from the moment I was at Hi Tops to the next morning waking up in Darron's apartment.

I stayed in my room for three solid days. My mom came to my door, asking what was wrong, but I couldn't tell her because I didn't even know how to process what did or did not happen to me. The whole ordeal, I felt, was making me crazy.

I came to a crossroads: Should I continue to mentally beat myself up about something I would never have answers to, or should I just let go of the concern and pretend this never happened? I decided the only way to press forward was to stuff the events of the night deep down inside of me and move on.

I did not realize that I started living in a constant state of fear, looking over my shoulder all the time for that awful guy. For almost an entire year, I never told a soul about that frightful experience I went through.

Almost a year later, my boyfriend (now husband), Brett, and I were driving down a country road to a friend's engagement party when I saw what looked like Darron's car pass us. Without even realizing it, I gasped loudly in fear. Brett immediately asked what was wrong. I tried to play it off and act like it was nothing, but Brett could clearly see I was shaken. Being the loving man he is, he encouraged me to tell him what was wrong. He pulled the car over, and we talked and talked and talked.

I had no idea how deeply that awful night was haunting me until I told all of it to Brett. Releasing all those emotions was exactly what I didn't even realize I needed. Those moments of talking to Brett about every bit of the incident allowed me to no longer feel trapped and alone in fear.

Although we never found out the exact details of that night, I was set free from emotional bondage. My mind had released its nightmare and God allowed Brett to help carry this burden for me. The Bible says in Galatians 6:2 (CSB), "Carry one another's burdens; in this way you will fulfill the law of Christ." God Himself took from me the torment of my unknown, for He knows everything. It says in 1 John 3:19–20 (CSB), "This is how we will know that we belong to the truth and will reassure our hearts before him whenever our hearts condemn us; for God is greater than our hearts, and He knows all things."

Twenty-five years later, Brett and I were settling into our seats on a plane headed for a nice little vacation. I grabbed my phone to switch it to airplane mode and noticed I had a text from my brother telling me that Darron recently died of an aneurysm. A flood of emotions rushed over me, and I found myself in tears. Brett hugged me and asked if I was okay. I told him that guiltily, I felt a huge relief by Darron's death, but intertwined were concerns for his salvation. I realized that somewhere along the way, I had forgiven Darron. I was hoping Darron had come to know Christ as his Savior, so he did not face the scary alternative. The Bible says in Romans 6:23 (CSB), "For the wages of sin is death, but the gift of God is eternal life in Christ Jesus our Lord."

I was and still am so thankful to our loving Lord for knowing exactly what I needed in order to free myself from this nightmare. He provided that in Brett by giving me a man who wouldn't let me hold on to a haunting moment that I had no control over. A man who wouldn't let me live in entrapment. A man who showed me he would gently carry my heart and walk with me through fearful moments, never allowing me to push down things I needed to deal with. A man who, through Christ's guidance, showed me how to rid my mind of torture.

Most importantly, I am forever thankful to the Lord for allowing me to forgive someone I equated with evil.

We are not meant to carry hardships on our own. God gives us people in life to share the good and the bad. He does this to mirror how we are to lay our burdens at His feet. He wants to take them from us, teach us, and allow us to grow in the process.

God took care of me in such a tender way all those years ago and still does to this day. If you find yourself at a crossroads of holding onto something that you have no control over, I encourage you to release it to God. The Bible says in 1 Peter 5:7 (NIV), "Cast all your anxiety on him because he cares for you." He *will* carry your burden for you and redeem what was broken or lost. There is freedom in giving God your confusion or hurt. Trust Him. I had to and am free because of it.

"Now to him who is able to do immeasurably more than all that we ask or imagine […] to him be glory." Ephesians 3:20–21 (NIV)

Prayer:

Dear Lord, thank You, thank You, thank You! Thank You for knowing every detail of our lives and always being ready to take our hurt away. Thank You for Your promises of never leaving us and freeing us from any type of bondage. Provide for us people in our lives who we can trust to carry our burdens with us and talk us through our hardships. Most importantly, may our trust in You and understanding of You be greater than our fear of holding on. In Jesus' name, we pray, amen.

Questions:

What thoughts or emotions rose up as you read this story?

How are you letting God take from you your hurt or confusion over something upsetting you have been through or are going through? Matthew 11:28–29 (ESV) says, "Come to me, all who labor and are heavy laden, and I will give you rest. Take my yoke upon you, and learn from me, for I am gentle and lowly in heart, and you will find rest for your souls."

Your story may be unlike my story. But each of us goes through hardships in life that ultimately lead us to a crossroads of trusting God or holding onto hurt. Ask God now to allow you freedom by placing your heartache in His hands.

Write down things you are holding onto that are taking your thoughts captive. Pray over them daily until you feel Him allowing you to let go and forgive.

A Step Closer:

Here are some Scripture verses pertaining to peace that come from God: John 16:33, John 14:27, 2 Thessalonians 3:16, 1 Peter 3:10–11, Psalm 4:8, Isaiah 26:3, Colossians 3:15, and Jude 1:2.

Here are some Scripture verses about anxiety: John 14:27, 2 Timothy 1:7, Psalm 55:22, Philippians 4:6, Hebrews 13:6, and Joshua 1:9.

**If you have experienced some sort of violation and have never spoken about it, I encourage you to pray for God to provide a safe person to share it with. Once I experienced what I did, I understood why so many women keep quiet about what possibly happened to them. This chapter was difficult for me to share, but I am hoping it will ultimately encourage others to be able to piece together whatever they went through, talk about it, and trust God to take it from them, freeing them.

15

PRETTY PLEASE

As I was kneeling down, putting my toddler Olivia's squeaky shoes on so we could go on a bike ride, Cora timidly said, "Mama." I looked up and saw her three-year-old little body all dressed in her princess dress with her new sparkly shoes on. I knew what she wanted. I said, "Cora, you look precious, baby, but you know you cannot wear those shoes. They are your dress shoes and will fall off when you are peddling because they have no straps to hold them on your feet." She looked disappointed, but then her face brightened up. She said, "Wait, just a minute," and ran out of the room.

I continued to gather Olivia's sippy cup, snack bag, and baby doll. When I knelt down to scoop her up in my arms, I looked up and noticed Cora standing near the doorway with a big smile on her face. I glanced down to see if she had changed shoes. Nope. However, there were two rubber bands stretching across the middle of her feet, now holding her shoes on tightly. Amazed at her determination, I smiled and said, "Okay, that works for me. You can wear them." She excitedly skipped off ahead of Olivia and me and jumped on her bike.

This made me think of how God must view us when we come before Him with our sincere, heartfelt requests, no matter how silly they may seem. The Bible says to approach the throne with boldness in Hebrews 4:16 (ESV): "Let us then with confidence draw near to the throne of grace." And Matthew 7:7 (CSB) says, "Ask, and it will be given to you. Seek, and you will find. Knock, and the door will be opened to you." We are to come to our Father in prayer with anything and everything on our minds. He is a loving Father and wants us to communicate with Him.

Now, just because we ask for something doesn't mean He will give it to us. He is all-knowing and knows what is best for us. When I was in junior high and wished to marry the most popular singer in a boy band, God did not allow for that in my life, thankfully. God knew exactly who I needed in life to complete me and keep me striving for Jesus, and it was not anyone from New Kids On The Block.

What Cora presented at first did not work best for her and could cause her harm, so I would not accept it. However, when she stepped out of the room, made a change, and came back to ask me, my answer changed to a favorable yes. Ephesians 3:12 (NIV), says, "In him and through faith in him we may approach God with freedom and confidence."

We must check what we are asking God to see if it lines up with His will for our lives, and sometimes that might mean we have to make a change to our request or throw it out altogether. Jesus prayed in Luke 22:42 (ESV), "Father, if you are willing, remove this cup from me. Nevertheless, not my will, but yours, be done." Jesus still made His requests known to God but knew to end his prayer by ultimately requesting God's will to be done.

God wants to give us the desires of our hearts, but He is a wise, protective, loving Father who will not allow us to walk in harm's path. He sees the big picture and knows which avenues we should take and which ones we should avoid. Of course, there will be hardships along any path we choose, but those also eventually draw us closer to Him.

Once Olivia and I were finally cruising on the bike behind Cora, I was overjoyed as I watched Cora ride so happily with her sparkly shoes. She was proudly living out what her little heart had desired.

God does the same with us as He delights in watching us live life to the fullest, the way He has so graciously planned for us to live it. Psalm 149:4 (ESV)says, "For the Lord takes pleasure in his people; he adorns the humble with salvation." When we ask God first, we can then trust that He will place us in the center of His will, which is the best and safest place for us to be. It's where we thrive and enjoy all that He has made for us to enjoy. John 16:24 (ESV) says, "Until now you have asked nothing in my name. Ask, and you will receive, that your joy may be full."

Prayer:

Dear Lord Jesus, thank You for letting us come to You in prayer with anything and everything. Thank You for the times You have not given us what we asked for because You knew we deserved better. Let us come to welcome and trust Your provision and protection in our lives. In Jesus' name, we pray, amen.

Questions:

How did God speak to you as you read this story?

What specific things have you asked God for and now you know He protected you by not giving it to you?

What do you want to bring to God in prayer that maybe He is pressing upon your heart to change or to keep asking for?

A Step Closer:

Writing down Bible verses and placing them around your house serves as a protection. Here are some Scripture verses related to God's protection: Isaiah 54:17, 2 Thessalonians 3:3, Psalm 46:1, Deuteronomy 31:6, Isaiah 41:10, Psalm 34:7, and Psalm 32:7.

Here are some comforting Scripture verses pointing out how God delights in us: Zephaniah 3:17, Psalm 18:19, and Psalm 37:4.

Cora, Shilah, Brett, Priscilla and Olivia

16

Good Friday

I stood by the ICU entrance, peeking through the door in hopes of catching a glimpse of my father every time a nurse or an adult would walk in or out. I was told repeatedly that I could not go in because I was only twelve years old. My father was in the far right corner of the Intensive Care Unit, leaning up in his bed; he noticed me desperately looking at him.

He quickly called a nurse over, and sternly said something to her while motioning to the tubes attached to him. The nurse walked briskly over to me and quietly said, "Come with me." How overjoyed I was that the door and all the rules no longer confined me from seeing my father. I ran into his arms and hugged him so tightly and thanked him for making a way to come see him.

When I asked what he said to the nurse, he responded, "I told her, 'Look over in that doorway. You see that little girl? She is my daughter. If you do not let her come to me, I will rip every tube you have me hooked up to and walk out there and get her myself.'" I was so proud of my father and so thankful that he made a way for me to be with him.

One of my favorite verses in the Bible is Romans 8:38–39 (ESV). "For I am sure that neither death nor life, nor angels nor rulers, nor things present nor things to come, nor powers, nor height nor depth, nor anything else in all creation, will be able to separate us from the love of God in Christ Jesus our Lord."

Many months passed, and the day finally came for my father to be released to come home. As they wheeled him out of the hospital, the nursing staff clapped while they sang, "For he's a jolly, good fellow, for he's a jolly good fellow!" My father looked over to me and said, "Cheri, do you know what today is? It's Good Friday." Then he smiled so big and said, "It is a good Friday, indeed."

Every Good Friday, I think about the time in the hospital when I was restricted from being near my father, and he boldly made a way where there appeared to be no way. And I reflect on Christ making a way for us, His children, to be with Him by dying on the cross for our sins. As 1 Peter 3:18 (ESV) says, "For Christ also suffered once for our sins, the righteous for the unrighteous, that he might bring us to God, being put to death in the flesh but made alive in the spirit." I think of all the things *we think* separate us from Him. Yet, Jesus already broke the ties of sin that bound us. He did not let anyone or anything stand in His way to bridge the eternal gap between us and Him. "By this is love perfected with us, so that we may have confidence for the day of judgment, because as he is so also are we in this world" 1 John 4:17 (ESV).

We must remember that He is eagerly waiting for us to take the bold step of faith and walk towards Him. The Bible says in Hebrews 4:16 (CSB), "Therefore, let us approach the throne of grace with boldness, so that we may receive mercy and find grace to help us in time of need." May we truly surrender to Him and be grateful for the pathway He created for each of us to be with Him both now and forevermore. For *He* is indeed a jolly, *good* Fellow!

Prayer:

Dear Heavenly Father, let us have the faith of a child and approach You boldly knowing You accept us as is. Thank You for dying on the cross for us, ridding us of our sins and welcoming us in Your presence. And may we forever long to be near You, sweet Jesus. It's in Your name we pray, amen.

Questions:

What did God reveal to you as you read this story?

In what ways do you know that God is good?

What holds you back from approaching God with confidence in order to receive grace? We all need His grace.

A Step Closer:

Look up Matthew 18:3 and read what it says about what we should do to enter heaven and ask God to help you make the necessary changes in order to do so.

Here are some Scripture verses confirming what Christ did on the cross for us: 1 Peter 2:24, 1 Corinthians 15:3, Isaiah 53:5, John 3:16, Romans 5:8, John 19:30, and Romans 6:23.

> My cheri:
> The day that you can't write me little notes of love (from my #1 angel) will be the day that love is no more - and that day will never be.
>   I love you,
>   Dad

One of the many notes my daddy often left for me to find. I am so thankful I kept this!

17

NAKED AND AFRAID

As my daughters, Pippy and Olivia, ran ahead of me in the airport to go to the restroom once getting off the plane, I grabbed our belongings and eventually made my way to them. By the time I got to the restroom, my daughters were walking out, and they quietly came to me and said, "Mom, there's a lady in there who needs help." Their eyes were wide open, almost pleading with me to help the lady.

As I approached the opening of the restroom, many people had gathered around, laughing and eventually walking away, saying condescending things under their breath. I walked in and saw a lady wandering around completely topless near the sink area. She was clearly inebriated in some way or another and was at her rock bottom.

I walked up to her, placed my hands on her shoulders, and said, "Ma'am, do you need a shirt?" She nodded her head and weepily said, "Yes. Yes." She was very distraught and mumbling about some guy leaving her. I grabbed a spare sweatshirt that was in my bag, put that on, and handed her the shirt I was wearing. I told her it was going to be okay, and that Jesus loves her. I prayed for her and walked out of the restroom.

As I walked away from the scene, my daughters were waiting for me. I hastily told them to begin walking. They asked what happened, but I said nothing and just shook my head. I was angry. I was angry that nobody helped that poor lady and that everyone was more amused at her being a spectacle and something to joke about.

As my daughters and I walked on toward the exit, tears flowed down my face. I explained to them that when I saw that lady, she reminded me of a family member of ours who was battling with drug addiction. I asked my daughters how they would want people to treat our loved one if it were her in the bathroom. That made it very personal to each of us. I explained to them that we need to take advantage of opportunities like the one we just encountered to wrap Jesus's love around those of us who are found in difficult situations. Colossians 3:12 (NIV) says, "Therefore, as God's chosen people, holy and dearly loved, clothe yourselves with compassion, kindness, humility, gentleness and patience."

This instance made me wonder how many times my family member had been in a situation where she was stranded and afraid, and people chose to ridicule her instead of helping her. It broke my heart. Then, I wondered how many times in life I have been the one to walk past someone in dire need and chose to judge them instead of extending love to them. More than I'd like to know, I'm sure.

In the Bible, there was a similar story of a man who was beaten and left helpless on the side of the road. Many walked past him. Only one (a Samaritan) stopped to help the man. And it was clear the Samaritan did not help the beaten man in order to receive any kind of recognition but did it because it says he "had compassion" on him (Luke 10:33, CBS).

There is another story in the Bible that comes to mind, and that is the one that tells of the adulteress woman in the town square whom some wanted to cast their stones upon. Jesus handled this in the most brilliant way. Saying nothing, He wrote something in the dirt for all to see. Whatever He wrote shut the accusers up quickly, and they fled the scene. All is okay when pointing the finger at others' faults until the light shines upon our own sin, right? How can we, as sinful humans, cast judgment upon anyone ever, knowing that we have our own sins we must deal with?

I think of that lady from time to time. I wonder if she felt Jesus's love (not me) clothe her that day? As 1 John 4:16 (ESV) says, "So we have come to know and to believe the love that God has for us. God is love, and whoever abides in love abides in God, and God abides in him." I wonder if she was able to turn things around in her life and take hold of Jesus, the only Man who would never ever leave her here on this earth or beyond. I like to think that she did make positive changes in her life, and that she is now able to notice others struggling and show them a better way.

May our hearts be filled with compassion in such a way that causes us to reach out and help others with Jesus' love. May we never be too full of ourselves to realize that it could be us one day who are found alone, afraid, and in need of someone with genuine, godly love to help us. We are all just a few bad decisions away from being the one who is wandering around not knowing which way is up or what step to take next. Allow Jesus to free you from any fear that is holding you in bondage, and let Him clothe you in His grace and love.

"I rejoice greatly in the Lord, I exult in my God; for he has clothed me with the garments of salvation and wrapped me in a robe of righteousness." Isaiah 61:10 (CSB)

Prayer:

Please, Lord Jesus, take anything away from us that is lording over our lives other than You. Please wrap your forgiveness and love around us. And, Jesus, please forgive us for times when we have walked past those in need. Forgive us if we have laughed and ridiculed others when they were downtrodden. May we delight in You more than anything this world could possibly offer. Thank You for allowing us moments in life to be able to gently bring others in and extend Your love to them. May those be the things that fill our hearts with joy. May You receive all the glory. It's in Your precious Son's name we pray, amen.

Questions:

What did God reveal to you as you read this story?

What do you think God is trying to teach you from it?

Do you realize that there is *nothing* you can do or not do to make Jesus love you any less? In what ways does this comfort you?

Do you feel judged by others? Read these following verses and see what God says about judging others. Matthew 7:1–5 (ESV): "Judge not, that you be not judged. For with the judgment you pronounce you will be judged, and with the measure you use it will be measured to you. Why do you see the speck that is in your brother's eye, but do not notice the log that is in your own eye? Or how can you say to your brother, 'Let me take the speck out of your eye,' when there is the log in your own eye? You hypocrite, first take the log out of your own eye, and then you will see clearly to take the speck out of your brother's eye."

A Step Closer:

Here are some comforting verses displaying Christ clothing us in His righteousness and love: Job 29:14, Romans 13:14, Ephesians 4:24, 2 Corinthians 5:3, 2 Corinthians 5:21, and Ephesians 6:14.

Here are some verses about compassion: Exodus 33:19, Isaiah 30:18, Isaiah 49:10, Isaiah 49:13, Isaiah 54:10, Isaiah 63:7, James 5:11, and Lamentations 3:32.

18

SHOTGUN RIDER

WHEN I WAS FIFTEEN years old, you might have found me driving around town in my little red car, jamming out to whatever music was popular at the time. I loved all kinds of music and loved even more how cool it sounded when it was cranked all the way up. I was proud of my stereo system and the amazing CD collection I purchased with my hard-earned babysitting money.

One morning, not long after I had purchased my car and its cool sound system, I walked out my back door leading to our carport and stood frozen in disbelief. The doors and seats of my car were removed by the thieves, and my sound system was stolen. A feeling of violation crept over me. How could this be? We were *just* inside the door sleeping when someone snuck under our roof and took my belongings right under our noses. I soberly processed the fact that, if they wanted to, the thieves could have come in and attacked us. Quickly, I tried to shake those thoughts out of my mind and replace them with thoughts of gratitude by reminding myself that we were protected, and the only bad thing that happened was that my stereo system had been stolen.

After reporting the theft to the police, I had my seats placed back in my car and went on about my day. I doubt I had insurance that covered the stereo system because, for the next solid year, I drove around not only without a CD system but with no radio at all. Eventually, I put my old jambox in my car and rode around listening to the only cassette tape I had, which was *praise and worship* music.

I believe Jesus presented Himself to me in the most tender way while I was riding around in silence, or with only the sound of worship music. I literally felt

His peaceful presence with me in the car. The Bible says in 1 Peter 1:8–9 (NIV), "Though you have not seen him, you love him; and even though you do not see him now, you believe in him and are filled with an inexpressible and glorious joy, for you are receiving the end result of your faith, the salvation of your souls."

The same morning of the theft, I would have gone directly to the store and bought another stereo system if I could have afforded it. But that was not God's intention for me. I believe He had a time set aside for me to be silent. A time for me to listen. A time for me to learn how to recognize His presence, and a time to dwell in His peace. The Bible says in Ecclesiastes 3:1–7 (NIV), "There is a time for everything, and a season for every activity under the heavens: [...] a time to be silent and a time to speak." It may sound funny to you, but I remember a few times glancing over at the empty passenger seat and smiling, knowing He was riding with me.

Every one of us has the gift of unlimited access to Jesus' presence. We just need to ask for it and make ourselves available to Him. He places loving things in our hearts, guiding us the way He often does *when we allow time for Him*. When we invite Him into our lives every day, He floods our minds with clarity and our souls with contentment.

Through my stereo theft experience, I learned how God often will prune or cut away things in our lives that keep us from blossoming. I am not saying my sound system or my music was bad, harmful, or ungodly. I am saying that He wanted me to be still, quiet, and realize that in Christ, we are never alone. He knew what I needed and, in a unique way, provided it for me. Silence with Him spoke louder than music without Him.

The "thieves" who snuck under my carport that night meant bad for me, but God showed up and turned it into good. Genesis 50:20 says (ESV), "As for you, you meant evil against me, but God meant it for good."

Truth be known, once I had my stereo placed back in my car, I missed the quiet moments I used to have with Jesus. I missed the deeply rooted growth that took place in the stillness beside Him.

To this day, I try to slow down and turn down the noise in life, glance over at the empty seat beside me, and remember that Jesus is there with me and always has been my "Shotgun Rider."

"The thief comes only to steal and kill and destroy. I came that they may have life and have it abundantly." John 10:10 (ESV)

"The world cannot accept him, because it neither sees him nor knows him. But you know him, for he lives with you and will be in you." John 14:17 (NIV)

Prayer:

Dear Heavenly Father, thank You for your protection over us. Thank You for being a constant presence in our lives. Please help us give You the frightening moments in our lives and ask You to show us how they can be turned around for good, for Your glory. In Jesus' name, amen.

Questions:

What did God speak to your heart as you read this story?

In what ways have you felt Jesus' presence?

When have you had a bad situation become a teachable lesson for you to grow closer to Christ?

After reading these two verses, take a moment to reflect and write down how each speaks to you:

- John 20:29 (CSB): "Jesus said, "Because you have seen me, you have believed. Blessed are those who have not seen and yet believe."

- 2 Corinthians 4:18 (CSB): "So we do not focus on what is seen, but on what is unseen. For what is seen is temporary, but what is unseen is eternal."

A Step Closer:

Here are some Scripture verses that apply to stealing: 1 Corinthians 6:10, 1 Timothy 6:10, Ephesians 20:15, Exodus 22:7, Hosea 4:2, Leviticus 19:11, Leviticus 19:13, Luke 19:8, and Mark 10:19.

Here are some Scripture verses pertaining to restoration: Psalm 51:12, Isaiah 61:7, Galatians 6:1, Romans 8:19–21, Jeremiah 30:17, 2 Chronicles 7:14, Psalm 23:3, and Isaiah 61:3.

19

IN JUST A LITTLE WHILE

ONE OF THE HARDEST things for me to adjust to just after my daddy passed away was getting off the school bus at my Maw Maw's house and him not being there waiting on me.

Every day, the bus dropped me off there, and my daddy's tan van would be parked near her back carport. It comforted me knowing I would walk in and my daddy would be sitting at the kitchen table with his coffee, eating Maw Maw's homemade biscuits, with my Maw Maw sitting next to him chatting. I hugged them both, telling them all about my day as I reached into the fridge to grab the handle of the green glass pitcher filled with freshly brewed iced tea. After pouring a glass, I would sit in the empty chair next to Maw Maw and join in on the conversation.

When we finished with our coffee, tea and biscuits, Daddy and I kissed Maw Maw goodbye and hopped in his van to drive home. All the way home, my daddy talked to me about life. He was very intentional in teaching me and my siblings all about life and scenarios and how to be aware and prepared. He sometimes even said, "I won't always be here to do these things for you, so you need to learn now." I remember every time he said those things to us because it made me mad. Regardless, I paid attention, and I am now glad I did.

The first day of school after losing my daddy was gut-wrenching, and the afternoon bus ride was even worse. As the school bus started down the road to my Maw Maw's house, I remember feeling dread, not wanting to open my eyes because I knew what awaited me and what I would no longer see.

Sure enough, the bus brakes squeaked as it slowed to a stop. I grabbed my bag and walked down the aisle to the front. Step, step, step ... off the bus, and his van was not parked in its spot. My heart was crushed all over again. I slowly walked up the driveway, into the house, past the table where he would have been sitting, and into the kitchen to hug Maw Maw. I'm not sure if anyone could have prepared me for that moment. Needless to say, I went on about my day and days thereafter, regardless of how hard it was. Joshua 1:9 (ESV) says, "Have I not commanded you? Be strong and courageous. Do not be frightened, and do not be dismayed, for the Lord your God is with you wherever you go."

Not long after that first experience of the afternoon without my daddy, I had a dream. I dreamt I had just gotten dropped off by the bus and started down the driveway to my Maw Maw's house when I turned to see my daddy's van driving by. He was in his blue button-up shirt with his sleeves rolled up just a bit, waving to me, smiling so big. He said, "Tell Cheri I'll see her in just a little while."

I awoke quietly and sat with that moment. God had just given me a sweet message directly from my daddy, in such a tender way. God knew those days of getting off the bus were hard for me. So, He allowed me to see my daddy in his van, smiling and telling me that he would see me again. I held onto this precious dream and let the message sink deep into my heart and into my mind, and I have never let go of it.

You see, in heaven, time does not exist. I understood that. I understood this message from the Lord about my daddy. It was like my daddy was saying, "I am good, I am happy, and I *will* see you. You may have to wait long because you are bound by earthly time, but it won't be long for me."

The vision God gave me of my daddy changed my days of stepping off the bus at my Maw Maw's house. I understood clearly that I still had a life to live here, and my daddy was where he needed to be, and all would be made whole again ... one day.

The Bible says to never tire from doing what is right. Galatians 6:9 (ESV) says, "Let us not grow weary of doing good." Days can get long, and memories can be overwhelming at times because of the very fact that that's all they are—memories and no longer tangible moments. However, Jesus has walked me through all these valleys and helped me hold gratitude for the moments I did have with my daddy. Jesus has taught me to lean on His Word and not my own understanding and to not tire from living the life He has gifted me with. Proverbs 3:5 (ESV) says, "Trust in the Lord with all your heart, and do not lean on your own understanding." How sweet of the Lord to give me a clear picture of my daddy waiting for me.

As my husband and I were recently talking about my daddy, I said to him, "Do you know I am forty-six years old right now, and I lost my daddy at age thirteen? I was so fascinated with my daddy that there has not been one day that goes by that I do not think about him." My husband asked, "What is it that you think about?" I told him I think of all the things he took time out to teach us, to do with us, and to show us. I think of him dancing in the kitchen with my mom. I think of him making a swing and a treehouse for us, and working his tail off to bring us to see God's creations each summer. I think of him laughing while riding me through the backyard in the wheelbarrow. I think of what he would have loved about my husband and about my girls. I think of how I used to wrap my hand around his finger and hold on tight as he walked me across the street. I think of when he told me to go into the dentist's office and check myself in because one day, he wouldn't be there to do that for me. I think of how he taught me how to fish and shoot a gun and how he encouraged me to walk up the aisle in church to pray for my mom when she was going through a difficult time. I think of how he left little notes of love all throughout my room for me to find, just to let me know he cared. "I think of it all." I looked at my husband and said, "I guess I am still fascinated by him."

God has allowed me to not forget all the precious memories of my daddy and for me to be grateful for the daddy he gave to us. Philippians 1:3 (ESV) says, "I thank my God in all my remembrance of you." My daddy was not perfect, nor am I. But he was my daddy, and I was his little girl. If God needed to take him away when He did in order for Him to receive glory and for me to learn and grow closer to our heavenly Father, then I do not doubt God's plan for us. I am just thankful.

If your days have become long and painful, I encourage you to open God's Word and pray for Him to fill you with exactly what you need. He will do it, and He will do it in a personal way. He knows you and loves you and will meet you in your time of need because He is just that good!

"Let us then with confidence draw near to the throne of grace, that we may receive mercy and find grace to help in time of need." Hebrews 4:16 (ESV)

"But do not overlook this one fact, beloved, that with the Lord one day is a thousand years, and a thousand years as one day." 2 Peter 3:8 (ESV)

"And let us not grow weary of doing good, for in due season we will reap, if we do not give up. So then, as we have opportunity, let us do good to everyone, and especially to those who are of the household of faith." Galatians 6:9–10 (ESV)

Prayer:

"Dear Jesus, thank You for knowing our needs and meeting us exactly where we are. Thank You for comforting us in such personal ways. Help us to see You in every walk of life ... the good times and the tough times. We love you so much! In Your precious name, we pray, amen."

Questions:

What thoughts or emotions rose up as you read this story?

When have you noticed God reaching out and comforting you?

Can you take painful moments you've been through and notice that God was right there with you? Take a moment and ask Him to show you His presence and goodness in your life.

Explain how God has given you strength and grown you to trust Him through the tough times you endured.

A Step Closer:

Here are some Scripture verses encouraging you to keep going: Isaiah 40:31, Philippians 4:13, 1 Corinthians 15:58, Romans 8:28, Psalm 23:4, Hebrews 12:1–2, Isaiah 41:10, Psalm 27:14, and Philippians 3:14.

Here are some Scripture verses pertaining to visions and dreams: Genesis 15:1, Genesis 41:1–7, Genesis 46:2, Job 4:13–16, Exodus 3:2–3, Acts 7:30-32, Judges 7:13–15, 1 and Samuel 3:2–15.

Maw Maw Jackson's house where my daddy and I would meet after school. His van used to be parked on the left side of the house.

20

SINK

HEADING BACK TO OUR room after hours of swimming in the hotel pool, we stepped into the elevator. I pushed two-year-old Shilah in the little Winnie the Pooh stroller while Cora and Olivia stood close by Brett's side. The doors opened, and a man stepped on the elevator with us. Shilah, in her little red starfish swimsuit, looked up at him and said, "I didn't sink." He halfway glanced down at her and looked away again. She repeated herself. "I didn't sink." Brett, the girls, and I giggled and told Shilah we were very proud of her for not sinking and that she did a great job staying afloat. I imagine that in her sweet little mind, she recalled how all went well in the pool, and she was so proud of herself for not sinking.

Earlier, when all of us were swimming, Shilah had her eyes on her father the entire time. She was fixated on him, made a beeline in his direction, and swam to safety in his arms. No matter what was going on around her, like her sisters jumping in, splashing all around her, and playing pool games, Shilah remained focused and swam directly to her father.

Matthew 14:28–31 (ESV) says, "Peter answered [Jesus], 'Lord, if it is you, command me to come to you on the water.' He said, 'Come.' So Peter got out of the boat and walked on the water and came to Jesus. But when he saw the wind, he was afraid, and beginning to sink he cried out, 'Lord, save me.' Jesus immediately reached out his hand and took hold of him."

It was only when Peter took his eyes *off the Lord*, his Father, that he began to sink. Similarly, when Shilah kept her eyes locked on her father, she was able to make it safely to him. Back on the elevator, she was recalling her victory in swimming and not sinking by telling the man, "I didn't sink."

Shilah's focus reminded me of something that occurred just a couple of years prior to the elevator encounter. While Brett was busy at work (coaching for the New York Jets), I, along with our three daughters, were driving down the streets of Long Island, NY, headed to a dentist appointment. Having almost reached my destination, I received a call from Brett. As soon as I answered, he told me the Jets had fired him.

As he explained the shocking news to me, I drove past a church with a sign along the road that read, "Give thanks in *all* circumstances; for this is God's will for you in Christ Jesus" (1 Thessalonians 5:18, ESV). Immediately, I said to Brett, "We are to be thankful. This is a blessing that we cannot yet see." And, indeed, it was.

God did not allow one second to lapse between the time Brett told me he was fired and when I read the verse that soon comforted and directed us. We were not given even a moment to get downhearted or upset over the upsetting news we just received.

To explain this in my Mom's words, "God kept your eyes fixated on Him in order to allow your husband's heart to not become discouraged." God kept our eyes above water, not letting our focus on Him sink. In that instant, God called us to trust Him with our plans, beckoning us to look up and keep hope alive for our family's future.

Brett now says that leaving the Jets was the best thing that could have happened to his career. From New York, he went to Florida and worked with a company that taught him the science and the "why" behind strength and conditioning exercises. After gaining this wisdom, he went on to become a successful strength and conditioning coach for the Dallas Cowboys for close to ten years.

When we keep our eyes fixated on the Lord, it saves us in more ways than one. We keep in step on the path He has chosen for us to walk. He keeps us out of trouble and all kinds of danger, and He helps us not to sink into despair, emotionally or physically. No matter what is going on around us, when we breathe in

God's Word, hold tight to His promises, and ask Him to lead us, all will be well. Hebrews 12:1–2 (CSB) says, "Let us run with endurance the race that lies before us, keeping our eyes on Jesus, the pioneer and perfecter of our faith."

When we feel ourselves drowning with the weight of the world and notice our focus shifts off of Him, we must take a second to ask the Lord to redirect our attention back to Him. All Peter had to do was cry out to Jesus, and the Bible says he was *immediately* saved. Jesus is always there, waiting for us with open arms, ready to rescue us when we call upon Him.

In order to keep your grounding throughout life, you must have a focal point; you must have an unwavering, steady object to look at. Hebrews 13:8 (ESV) says, "Jesus Christ is the same yesterday and today and forever." Christ is unchanging. He is the *only* one in life that you can trust to never alter His Word, His promises, His love, His presence, His comfort, His kindness, and everything that makes Him who He is. All we have to do is keep our eyes locked on Jesus, our heavenly Father, and dive safely into His arms. Then, just like Shilah did all those years ago, we can rejoice in our victory of not sinking.

Prayer:

Dear Lord Jesus, thank You for always beckoning us to You with Your arms stretched out wide. Thank You for being our immediate help in time of need. May we keep our focus on You and not fixate on the troubles of this world. And may we enjoy being in the presence of Your loving arms. In Jesus' name, we pray, amen.

Questions:

How did God speak to you as you read this story?

In what ways do you feel you are sinking in life?

Write about a moment in time when you called out to Jesus and He rescued you.

A Step Closer:

Here are some Scripture verses about focusing on God: Psalm 16:8, Colossians 3:2, Proverbs 4:25, Hebrews 12:2, Psalm 141:8, Philippians 4:8, 1 Chronicles 16:11, Psalm 25:15, and Psalm 105:4.

Here are some Scripture verses telling how God is never changing: Psalm 102:27, Malachi 3:6, James 1:17, Daniel 7:14, and Hebrews 1:12.

SINK

Shilah and Brett

21

Down the Aisle

It was my brother.

It was my brother who was pushing me in the shopping buggy as fast as he could up and down the aisles of the grocery store while Mama shopped quietly on another aisle. Shortly after this ride, you could hear the worker come over the loudspeaker saying, "Clean up on aisle two. Karo syrup spill." Somehow or another, it was right then my brother and I found ourselves walking quietly alongside our mother, who wondered what could have taken place on aisle two.

It was my brother who pulled me behind the riding lawnmower on a piece of plywood around the neighborhood like we were in some kind of parade.

It was my brother who rode me on the handlebars of his bike, and we went flying through the air, tumbling on the concrete when we popped a wheelie and landed wrong.

It was my brother who taught me how to shoot with a pellet gun. In the front yard, we shot out streetlights. In the backyard, it was squirrels. We skinned the squirrels and kept the tails as souvenirs.

It was my brother I skipped school with to go mud riding in a local park, and I almost flew out of the truck when we hit a hidden ditch going full speed.

It was my brother who would ride me through the back trails in the neighborhood on the back of his dirt bike, and I learned to hold on for dear life or else.

It was my brother who taught me how to gleek, how to frog someone, and how to jump off the roof onto our rope swing in the backyard.

It was my brother who brought me to middle school in his super high-lifted black truck that made humming sounds when we drove up to the car line. I felt so cool being with him in his truck.

It was my brother who stopped me just before we walked down the aisle of the funeral home at my daddy's service and asked me, "Are you okay? Are you ready for this, Cheri? I'll be right here with you."

It was my brother who prepped me for high school with all the talks. He made sure I knew how to speak like a lady, carry myself with respect, and demand it from others.

It was my brother who drove all the way to Destin, Florida, to rescue me and my friend who ignorantly drove there on spring break as fifteen-year-olds on a whim, without letting any adults know.

It was my brother who walked me down the field and presented me on the homecoming court in high school. He stood in my father's place.

It was my brother who pumped me up before I went to NFL cheerleading tryouts, telling me, "Walk in there knowing that you're going to nail it and with the confidence that your spot is secure on the team and that you're not going to let anyone take that from you!"

It was my brother who walked me down the aisle of the big, beautiful church where I got married to my best friend. As I held onto my brother's arm, I could feel the strength that I needed from him. He, again, stood in my father's place.

It was my brother who told hospice to go home and that he wanted to be the one to take loving care of Mama in her last days.

It has been my brother all along. The Bible says in Proverbs 17:17 (ESV), "A friend loves at all times, and a brother is born for adversity." This means that through all the stages in life, you are given a brother to trek it with.

You may not have a brother or a sister but look around. God surely has provided someone or lots of people to walk through life with. I was blessed to have a brother and sister and cousins who walked life side by side with me. Or maybe it is you who is the one making all the difference in someone else's life. There is always someone who needs to feel God's love or to be led to Jesus.

I am blessed to still have my brother by my side, even though we live four states away from each other. Truth be known, I have no idea who I would be without my brother and all of his love, encouragement, and support throughout my years.

My husband described my brother perfectly. "I have never met someone who wakes up each and every day and never thinks of himself. He puts everyone else before him in all he does." This exemplifies 1 Peter 4:9 (ESV). "Show hospitality to one another without grumbling."

I thank God for knowing exactly what I needed in life and giving me my brother. Romans 12:10 (ESV) says to "love one another with brotherly affection. Outdo one another in showing honor." There is no doubt in my mind that when my brother enters heaven, his house will be one of the biggest on the hill, and even then, I'm quite sure he'll be trying to bless someone else with it.

"It is more blessed to give than to receive." Acts 20:35 (ESV)

"Whoever brings blessing will be enriched, and one who waters will himself be watered." Proverbs 11:25 (ESV)

"The wicked borrow and do not repay, but the righteous give generously." Psalm 37:21 (CSB)

"Freely you received, freely give." Matthew 10:8 (CSB)

Prayer:

Dear Heavenly Father, thank You for providing for us people who are extensions of Your love. Let us recognize them and be appreciative of them. May each of us also be Your hands and feet, reaching out to others who need a constant encourager by their side. Thank You, Lord Jesus, for being our forever Friend. In Your name, we pray, amen.

Questions:

What memory came up for you as you read this story?

Do you have people in your life who have helped you along the way? Call out their names now and thank God for them.

Can you think of people God placed in your life you can reach out to and pour Christ's love into?

A Step Closer:

Here are some Scripture verses that reflect upon being there for one another: 1 Thessalonians 5:11, Philippians 2:1–7, 1 Corinthians 12:26, Romans 12:15, Hebrews 10:24, Hebrews 3:13, Ephesians 4:32, and John 15:12.

Here are some Scripture verses encouraging a Christlike attitude: Leviticus 19:18, Leviticus 19:34, Psalm 133:1, Proverbs 17:9, Proverbs 24:17–18, Matthew 5:41–42, Matthew 10:41–42, and Matthew 19:19.

My brother displaying his collection
of squirrels in our backyard.

22

Presence

One of my favorite childhood memories is when my daddy drove up our driveway in his police car and spoke my name over his intercom. I would look out our screen door, jumping up and down in excitement, looking into his smiling face as he watched me. I loved hearing my daddy call my name to let me know he was home. He would park his car, get out, bend down, and let me run into his arms. Being in a father's arms is a place of safety. I could feel love wrapping around me in his hug.

One evening, when my daddy was working night shifts, my mom was cooking dinner while my brother, sister and I were playing in the kitchen. I noticed a man walking briskly up our driveway, heading straight towards our door. Through the screen door, I could see this stranger approaching from far away, getting closer and closer. I said, "Mama, there's a strange man walking up our driveway." She turned around to see him and rushed to close our wooden door, sealing it shut with the deadbolt. The man beat on the door and screamed for us to let him in. He made up some story that his car had broken down and that he needed to use our phone. My mom yelled back, telling him to go use a neighbor's phone. He kept banging on the door, becoming angrier and angrier that we would not let him in. When he realized he could not persuade us, he left.

I watched him through the window as he walked away. He did not go to any of our neighbors' homes and plead to use their phones for help, nor did I see his "broken down car" anywhere. I knew then the man meant harm to us.

With my daddy being a police officer, he would call us every now and then when there was an escaped prisoner on the loose. He warned us to lock the doors and not go outside until he said it was safe. Our neighborhood was located in a place where the prisoners would trek through once they escaped. So, I thought to myself that maybe this was one of the prisoners who had broken out and saw an opportunity to break into our home.

When my daddy was home, nobody ever dared approach our home with his police car sitting in the front yard. His presence at our home made them pass our house by. I felt safe when he was home, knowing we were protected. Realizing this made me wonder how many times in our lives our heavenly Father has protected us without us even knowing.

My daddy's police car no longer sits in my driveway; however, our heavenly Father's presence surrounds us and abides with us in our home. As Christians, we can feel safe and protected knowing that the Lord Himself watches over us. Psalm 121:7–8 (NIV) says, "The Lord will keep you from all harm—he will watch over your life; the Lord will watch over your coming and going both now and forevermore." He goes before us, protecting our every step and lovingly guiding us down our chosen path.

I am thankful God blessed me with an earthly father who showed me unconditional love and protection. Unfortunately, not all of us have been blessed in this manner. Some people may feel anything but safe in their father's presence. May any of you who feel this way come to know Jesus as your gentle, caring Father, and let Him fill the void in your life that your earthly father failed to provide.

Revelation 1:8 (ESV) says, "'I am the Alpha and the Omega,' says the Lord God, 'who is and who was and who is to come, the Almighty.'" Genesis 17:1 (CSB) says, "I am God Almighty. Live in my presence and be blameless." Psalm 91:1 (CSB) says, "The one who lives under the protection of the Most High dwells in the shadow of the Almighty." The Bible repeatedly describes the Lord as having unwavering love for us and that He provides constant protection over us. When we ask Jesus into our hearts and into our lives, we are then able to rest in

His encompassing love. May we find our "home" to be in the peaceful presence of our heavenly Father, Jesus Christ.

"Because you have made the Lord—my refuge, the Most High—your dwelling place, no harm will come to you; no plague will come near your tent. For he will give his angels orders concerning you, to protect you in all our ways." Psalm 91:9–11 (CSB)

"The Lord protects you; the Lord is a shelter right by your side. The sun will not strike you by day or the moon by night." Psalm 121:5–6 (CSB)

Prayer:

Thank You, Lord Jesus, for being our Almighty Protector. Please continue to protect us, and may we feel Your presence and rest in it. Thank You for allowing us to leave everything at Your feet and be able to sleep peacefully. In Jesus' name, amen.

Questions:

What thoughts or emotions rose up as you read this story?

In what ways have you witnessed God protecting you?

List ways you feel frightened or afraid and give it to God by asking Him to protect you and replace those feelings of fear with His presence.

A Step Closer:

Here are a few Scripture verses that relate to our protection provided by the Lord: 2 Thessalonians 3:3, Psalm 46:1, Deuteronomy 31:6, Isaiah 41:10, Psalm 34:7, and Psalm 32:7.

Here are a few Scripture verses about the devil fleeing: James 4:7, Job 26:13, Nahum 3:17, 2 Timothy 2:22, 1 Thessalonians 5:22, and Proverbs 28:1.

Cheri and friend playing outside in the snow.
Cheri's daddy's police car parked just to the left.

23

WAVES

IT WAS A LOVELY summer day, and the Bech's were enjoying time together on the water, boat riding. All the family members were packed in two separate boats. It just so happens there was one boat mostly filled with adults while the other boat had Brett, me, our three young daughters, and lots of young nieces and nephews. Some of us were jumping in the water, swimming with dolphins. However, the weather changed suddenly. We felt a gust of cold air, and the wind picked up instantly. As we looked around, we saw dark, gray clouds headed toward us. The storm was directly between us and our land destination. We all agreed to hurry and head back ashore.

While on the ride back, sheets of rain slapped us in the face relentlessly like little, cold pellets. The waves grew large, causing our boat to rise and fall, crashing hard onto the water. This caused panic amongst all of us, but mostly the children. They were all looking directly into Brett's and my eyes, trying to decipher if they should be scared or not. Brett, as always, stayed calm and pressed forward with his task of bringing us safely to shore. I gathered the two youngest toddlers in my arms and huddled under a tiny table near the back of the boat.

It seemed as though we were never going to make it back to dry land. I was trying to scream so Brett could hear me asking him to pull over to the nearest dock and let us wait it out. He disagreed and said we needed to take this storm head-on and go as fast as we could to get out of it. I felt so vulnerable with all the little ones in our care. As I was trying to keep all the kids calm and hunkered down to the floor, I desperately prayed for God to keep us safe because, from the looks of it, there was no end to this storm in sight.

While praying, I suddenly remembered a song the girls and I often sang in the truck about Jesus calming the storm. I began singing it or more like screaming it. Brett and the girls joined in. As soon as those words to the song came out of our mouths, peace fell over all of us, and the storm broke immediately! We looked in the sky, and directly before us, God had painted a bright, beautiful rainbow. Matthew 8:27 (NIV) says, "The men were amazed and asked, 'What kind of man is this? Even the winds and the waves obey him!'"

We made it! We were safe! I was overcome with gratitude to our Savior. He literally saved us in such a terrible storm. God brought us through that storm as soon as and only when we turned our focus to Him. Just like when Peter in the Bible placed his focus on Jesus, he was rescued. When he cried out for God to save him, Jesus *immediately* saved him. Matthew 14:29–31 (NIV) says, "'Come,' he said. Then Peter got down out of the boat, walked on the water and came toward Jesus. But when he saw the wind, he was afraid and, beginning to sink, cried out, 'Lord, save me!' Immediately Jesus reached out his hand, caught him."

When Brett, the girls, and I started singing to Jesus, calling out to Him, His help came immediately. So many times throughout my girls' lives, they have remembered the storm God brought us through. It has given them peace to recall how visible His help was in a situation where everything was out of our control. Some may read this story and call it a coincidence. But you cannot convince any of us who experienced it that God was not the reason for our peace and safety.

It's when we try to tackle life on our own without our focus being on our help from above that all goes haywire. Jesus is always there, just one prayer (or song) away, patiently waiting for us to call upon Him for help. And when we truly cry out to God, be prepared for Him to show up.

Prayer:

Dear God, please keep our focus on You no matter if we are in a visible storm or a storm within ourselves. May we never lose the marvel of You and of all Your power and mercy and the evidence of Your faithfulness. Thank You, loving Father, amen.

Questions:

What did God speak to your heart as you read this story?

When has Jesus brought peace to you in the midst of a storm you were going through?

Read Psalm 121:1–2 (NIV): "I lift my eyes to the mountains—where does my help come from? My help comes from the Lord, the Maker of heaven and earth." How do you know this verse to be true in your life?

A Step Closer:

Take a moment to write down what life storm you recently went through, are currently going through, or one you may see ahead. Pray over what you have written, giving it to the Lord and thanking God if He brought you through it. Pray over it daily if you are currently walking through it. Pray without ceasing if you anticipate a storm ahead, asking Him to prepare you.

Here are some Bible verses about keeping our eyes on the Lord: Psalm 101:3, Psalm 119:18, Psalm 119:37, Isaiah 26:3, Hebrews 12:2, Philippians 4:8, Matthew 6:22, and Psalm 141:8.

Cora and Olivia and two of their lifelong friends in the ocean with a storm on the horizon.

24

GET UP AND GO

BRETT HAD JUST BEEN let go from the coaching staff of the New York Jets, so we bought a house back in Louisiana and waited to see where God would take us next. Although we were faithfully praying for a job, it seemed like months and months before an offer came.

In God's true fashion, Brett got about three job offers within one week. God is a gentleman and does not force His way upon you, so He often gives you options. He allows you choices so you will prayerfully consider each one and place it before Him, seeking His blessing. Isaiah 30:21 (NIV) says, "Whether you turn to the right or to the left, your ears will hear a voice behind you, saying, 'This is the way; walk in it.'"

After receiving the job offers, we looked into each one carefully. The offer that jumped out to me was for Brett to be a performance specialist in Gulf Breeze, Florida, at the Andrews Institute. I found it interesting to feel so strongly that Brett should accept this position, considering it was three states away from our hometown. Why would I be eager to move again and away from family while having three young ones to care for? One of the other job offers would allow us to stay in our hometown, but it didn't seem to be the right fit for reasons I could not pinpoint. Nevertheless, we kept praying faithfully that God would confirm where He wanted us next.

I was constantly praying over our situation and kept feeling more and more certain that God was calling us to Gulf Breeze, Florida. Soon, Brett was asked to drive to Florida for an official interview at the Andrews Institute, so we all hopped in the truck and headed to Florida. Brett dropped the girls and me off at a friend's house along the way, which was about an hour away from Gulf Breeze. My friend, who is a very strong Christian, suggested we all pray for Brett as he was interviewing. Brett, of course, did not know this because he wasn't with us. One thing we asked of God was to surround Brett with solid, Christian men who would daily encourage each other in their walk with the Lord.

About an hour later, Brett called to let me know how his interview went. He explained that it all went great, and then he said, "It's kind of interesting. It seemed like everyone there I met was a Christian, even the elderly lady at the front desk." As soon as he said that, I knew it was another confirmation that God was indeed calling us to move to Florida.

The director of Athletes' Performance at the Andrews Institute was Alex Martin. He was the one who was supposed to escort Brett around, as he would be the one doing the hiring. However, Alex was not there that particular day, so his assistant, Miles Kur, met with Brett and showed him around.

The next week, Brett was asked to drive to a town about two hours away from our hometown for the third job interview. This third prospect seemed like a great place for us to be, considering it would allow our children to attend a Christian school tuition-free. With this job, we would be surrounded by many sweet Christian families, some of whom we already knew. Lastly, this job opportunity provided a wonderful position that Brett would have been great at as the head coach of the football team. After Brett's last interview and tour of the school, we had dinner alongside the president of the school.

Brett and I quietly walked back to our room and were both a bit silent as we pondered the details of our visit. Finally, as we were settling into bed, he said, "I don't think this is where we are meant to be." I felt relieved and told him I felt the same way. At that moment I refrained from telling him I was still convinced we were supposed to move to Gulf Breeze. I trusted God would bring that truth to Brett in His timing.

On our long drive home on a bit of a desolate road, Brett slowed down. I did not know what he was doing, as there were no turns or reasons for him to slow down. He told me, "I've been praying for God to give me a sign specifically on the next license plate I see, an answer as to where we should move. When I was done praying, I looked and saw the license plate on this car (pointing to the car driving beside us). Look at it." The license plate read, "4021 KUR." Kur was the last name of the guy Brett had met with in Gulf Breeze just weeks before. Needless to say, we were shocked! That was undoubtedly another confirmation for us to know without question where God was leading our family next.

Brett was still considering all the job opportunities presented to him while I was itching to move and begin our new chapter of life in Florida. However, selecting a new position away from home was a big decision, and I respected Brett for not being irrational and wanting certainty.

During this time, I had begun homeschooling our two oldest daughters. I was teaching them history in a book entitled *History for Little Pilgrims.* Little did I anticipate the story lesson for that day was on Abraham and how God told him to get up and move his family. Genesis 12:1 shows that Abraham did not yet know where God was leading him. He was just supposed to obey and go. Genesis 12:1 (NIV) says, "The Lord had said to Abram, 'Go from your country, your people and your father's household to the land I will show you.'" This resonated with me deeply as God was telling Abram to move away from family and his hometown and that he was just supposed to trust that God knew what He was doing.

Near the bottom of the lesson were questions to answer. One of the questions asked, "How about you? Is God telling you to move and start anew somewhere? Are you trusting Him and obeying?" Tears rushed to my eyes as I read this question. How can God be so present in all the details of my little life? And how can He remain so patient with us? I quickly took a picture of the lesson's question and sent it to Brett.

A few days after that confirmation, I headed to the gym, leaving Brett at home to prepare breakfast for the girls. As I was running on the treadmill, Brett called me. He said, "You are not going to believe what just happened. Olivia (who was only six years old at the time) said, "Daddy, I know what Alex Martin looks like." I asked her how she knew, and she said, "I saw it in my mind, and y'all were doing this (motioning lifting weights). As soon as she said this, my phone started vibrating in my pocket. I grabbed it to see who was calling. It was Alex Martin calling me to say I got the job!"

We later asked Olivia what she saw in her mind. She said that her Daddy and Alex were lifting weights and that Alex had brown hair and a white shirt on with black shorts. What is interesting about this is that the only time Olivia had ever heard the name Alex Martin was about six months prior to this day, and he had never even called Brett. Furthermore, none of us had ever met or even seen Alex. When Brett finally met Alex, he was exactly as Olivia described him, except he was wearing a black shirt with white shorts.

This made me think of these two Scripture verses in the Bible referring to children and their faith: Matthew 18:2–4 says, "He called a small child and had him stand among them. 'Truly I tell you,' he said, 'unless you turn and become like little children, you will never enter the kingdom of heaven. Therefore, whoever humbles himself like this child—this one is the greatest in the kingdom of heaven.'" Matthew 19:14 (CSB), says, "Jesus said, 'Leave the little children alone, and don't try to keep them from coming to me, because the kingdom of heaven belongs to such as these.'"

In the Bible, Gideon also needed to be reassured multiple times before obeying God regarding the job He placed before him. Judges 6:39–40 (NIV) says, "Then Gideon said to God, 'Do not be angry with me. Let me make just one more request. Allow me one more test with the fleece, but this time make the fleece dry and let the ground be covered with dew.' That night, God did so. Only the fleece was dry; all the ground was covered with dew."

God knew Brett needed to be reassured that taking the job and moving his family to Florida was the right thing to do. When Brett and I called out in prayer, God answered, not once, not twice, but at least three times. The Bible describes God's character in Exodus 34:6 (NIV): "The Lord, the Lord, the compassionate and gracious God, slow to anger, abounding in love and faithfulness." God is patient with us. He knew what we needed and how to make us feel certain we were going to be smack dab in the middle of His will. So, off we went to become Floridians.

Prayer:

Dear Lord Jesus, thank You for having a perfect plan already laid out for us. Thank You for being patient with us in our time of uncertainty. Please let us never stop seeking Your wisdom and guidance. May we trust and obey and go when You say go. Thank You, sweet Jesus! In Your name, we pray, amen.

Questions:

What did God reveal to you as you read this story?

How are you actively seeking to be in the center of God's will?

In what ways are you stepping out in faith and trusting God with your future?

A Step Closer:

Here are some Scripture verses about God's confirmations: Psalm 119:106, Philippians 1:7, Hebrews 2:3, Deuteronomy 19:15, Hebrews 6:16, Acts 15:27, Esther 9:29, 2 Peter 1:10, and Mark 16:20.

Here are some Scripture verses about stepping out in faith: 2 Corinthians 5:7, James 2:14–24, 1 Peter 3:15, Psalm 119:105, Luke 9:57-58, Jeremiah 29:11–14, James 1:22, and Isaiah 42:16.

Priscilla was born in Gulf Breeze, Florida and here she is enjoying the beach there.

25

CALM

As my husband and I drifted peacefully off to sleep one summer evening, I awoke, realizing I could barely move due to exhaustion. I felt my heartbeat pumping all the way through my body. I remember looking down at my leg and seeing it move as the pulse desperately tried to push blood through my body. I faintly reached my arm over to tap Brett on his shoulder, waking him. With my eyes half shut, I softly said, "I don't feel right." Brett, thinking quickly, reached for my wrist and took my pulse. He jumped up, swooped me up in his arms, and rushed me out to his truck. He placed me in the passenger seat and took off for the hospital. All the way, I couldn't talk. I was so weak. He carried me into the waiting room, and they quickly admitted me in for testing, for I'd just been released from surgery (laparoscopic hysterectomy) the day before from the same hospital.

After a couple of hours of testing and waiting for results, I told a nurse I was going to go back home to get some sleep. The doctor immediately showed up in our room, telling us we could not leave. He said, "You have a pulmonary embolism. You have a blood clot in your lungs." He explained what that meant. When there is a blood clot present in one of your lungs, it does not stay there. It circulates throughout your bloodstream, eventually going through your heart. It can *block* the blood trying to reach your heart, and you can die instantly. He told us they needed to start injecting me with blood thinners immediately.

When he left the room, Brett called my mom, who was at my house already because she was helping me recover from my surgery. Brett told her what was going on and that they were admitting me.

Once they settled me into a room and had me all hooked up to the IV, the doctor came in. I was lying in the bed, holding Brett's hand as he sat next to me in a chair. The doctor said, "Do you know what all this means?" We answered, "Yes." He said, "You can die any second. How can you be so calm?" Brett and I both explained to him that we have faith in Jesus Christ and that we trust Him as my Healer and my Sovereign Lord. He will take care of me. The doctor looked at us in disbelief and left the room.

I looked over at my stoic husband and said, "Will you please pray over me?" He said so lovingly, "I have been praying over you this whole time. I haven't stopped."

The time in the hospital was so peaceful for me. God's presence filled my room—filled my soul. It seemed as though every nurse who came in to tend to me, every movie on TV, every show, every song somehow or another all related to Jesus. In those tender moments, Jesus was showing me that, just like my husband, He never stopped holding my hand. Jesus never left me.

Praise be to God that through lots of medical care and medicine, I was eventually able to become "embolism free." For one year, I gave myself shots of blood thinners and went to a blood doctor weekly to have my levels checked. Now, when I pass by that doctor's office, I thank God for healing me and letting me stay and do my job here in raising our four lovely daughters to know and trust in Christ. And when I work out, I think about this time in my life when I was too weak to exercise and had to wait patiently to regain my strength. And before I begin, I give that workout to God, thanking Him that I am physically able to exercise again.

During that unpredictable time, an overwhelming amount of peace flooded mine and Brett's hearts; we were never once worried. God took that from us because we let Him. We trusted in Him. The Bible says in Psalm 50:15 (ESV), "Call upon me in the day of trouble; I will deliver you, and you shall glorify me." God did just that. He delivered us from fear and worry and anxiety.

Truth be told, we will all find ourselves in situations where we will have the chance to panic or to give our present *blockade* to God. May we trust what the Bible says in Isaiah 41:10 (ESV): "Fear not, for I am with you; be not dismayed, for I am your God; I will strengthen you, I will help you." May we surround ourselves with firm believers who never stop praying for us and who jump, without hesitation, at the chance to help us. And, most importantly, may we *know* the One who rescues us and heals us and give all glory and praise to Him.

I live each day thankful because, in all honesty, I shouldn't be here. He gifted me with the chance to continue loving my girls, my amazing husband, and my family. And for that, I am eternally thankful.

"In me [Jesus] you may have peace." John 16:33 (ESV)

Prayer:

Dear Lord Jesus, thank You for all the times You have been our calming presence in the midst of confusion and uncertainty. The Bible says in Psalm 23, "You lead us beside still waters and restore our soul." You rescue us from things seen and things unseen. And we praise You for that! May our hearts remain grateful, and may we rejoice every day you gift us with. In Your precious name, we pray, amen.

Questions:

How did God speak to you as you read this story?

When have you felt God calming you in times when panic would normally set in?

A Step Closer:

Here are some Bible verses about calmness: Ephesians 4:26, James 1:19, 2 Timothy 1:7, Psalm 107:29–30, Matthew 8:23–27, John 14:1, John 14:27, and Psalm 37:7–9.

Here are some comforting verses highlighting God's mercy: Ephesians 2:4, Psalm 86:5, 2 Corinthians 1:3, Exodus 33:19, Micah 7:18, Psalm 52:8, Titus 3:5, and Romans 2:4.

Psalm 118:24 (ESV) says, "This is the day that the Lord has made; let us rejoice and be glad in it." What are you grateful for on this day?

Cora, Shilah, Olivia, and baby Priscilla working a lemonade stand at our home in Gulf Breeze, Florida. We pulled the lemons off of the tree on the side of our house. God allowed me to continue to enjoy moments like this with my family.

26

BABY BIRD EGGS

BRETT BARBEQUED FOR DINNER the first evening back in Texas after my mom's funeral service. I don't remember much about that night, but I do remember Brett excitingly calling us all outside to see a nest just near the back door that held four tiny blue bird eggs. The month was April, and new life was blooming all around.

We had just finished eating dinner. I was walking upstairs, lifting my phone to call my mom, just as I did every night at that time. I stopped halfway up the stairwell and felt as if a bomb had gone off in my chest. This was the first time I went to call her and realized she wouldn't be there to answer.

I dropped my arm down with the hand that held my phone and slowly walked upstairs toward my room, now feeling such a void in my life. I walked past my daughters' room, where I saw my third daughter, Shilah, sitting on her floor reading a book. I kept walking toward my bathroom. Turning the knob on to run my bathwater, I remembered my mom's words. "Cheri, it's going to be hard for you at times when you pick up your phone to call me. In those moments, I want you to place your phone down and call out to the Lord. Ask Him to fill you." So, there in my bathroom as my tub was filling with water, I knelt down and cried out for God to fill this aching hole in my heart.

Shortly after my bath, as I put on my facial creams, I yelled out for Shilah to come into my room with me because I felt lonely. I had never asked her anything like this before, but my sweet girl understood and kindly agreed. I asked Shilah if she would like me to read some of the books to her that she had been reading. She happily said yes and ran off to go get it.

Before I go any further in telling you what happened next, I must go back about a month in time to fill you in. When we were all in Louisiana gathered around my mom just before she passed, there was a sweet moment where it was just her and I sitting together. She smiled and looked over at me and said, "Isn't it neat of God to take me "home" around Easter time? I find it so interesting that He is bringing me "home" during a season that represents new life." I just hugged her and said, "Yes, ma'am." I did think it was cool because I knew Easter was her favorite holiday, and she loved the meaning of it.

Back to my room, where I sat with my eleven-year-old, I opened the book to read from the spot in which she left off. You must understand, before I go on, that Shilah had never read this book before, and I had not read it in at least five years or more.

The chapter was talking about two little girls playing together outside near a tree ... *during Easter time*. It mentioned how one of the little girls was comforting the other because a *family member had just passed away*. The sweet friend was listening to the other girl talk all about how she envisioned heaven to be for her loved one. The entire chapter was all about how we don't quite understand here what they fully understand up there (in heaven). The closing of the chapter talked about *eggs being in the nest* they had just found in the tree!

My jaw dropped. I looked up at Shilah, and her eyes were widened with amazement in what we just read. I put the book down, reached out, and pulled Shilah close to me, hugging her. I said, "Baby girl, God Himself just reached out of heaven and gave us a hug!" I explained to her how I was feeling earlier and how I had recently prayed for God to fill my aching void with His love.

In the Bible, God often uses the number three or repeats something three times in order to show emphasis or completion. He used three different instances in the exact chapter we were reading to show us His magnificent presence. It's as if He were saying, "I am here with you. See, I am intertwined in every detail of your life. I am wrapping my arms around you while you are hurting. I will not leave you."

The following days after this loving encounter with Christ, we watched as the baby bird eggs hatched. We celebrated new life as these precious creatures broke through the shells that once enveloped them. They were now free. Free to explore this new life they were unfamiliar with.

I couldn't help but think of Mom. I thought of her breaking through life here on earth into her new life in heaven. I thought of her opening her eyes in her beautiful, new environment and looking around in wonder at it all. Ephesians 3:20–21 (CSB) says, "Now to him who is able to do above and beyond all that we ask or think according to the power that works in us—to him be glory."

Mom was right. It was fascinating that God chose to take her "home" during Easter time. The Bible says in 2 Corinthians 5:17 (CSB), "Therefore, if anyone is in Christ, he is a new creation; the old has passed away, and see, the new has come!"

God took my brokenness and showed me how He pieces back our heartaches with His tender touch. His love and presence in my life are what glued my heart back together that evening. He continues to do so when I obey what my mom said so long ago, putting down everything else, reaching out, and asking God to fill me.

"I am the resurrection and the life. The one who believes in me, even if he dies, will live. Everyone who lives and believes in me will never die." John 11:25–26 (CSB)

Prayer:

Thank You, Heavenly Father, for comforting us in moments of despair and heartbreak. Thank You for showing us that You are our ever-present help. Thank You, most importantly, for dying on the cross for our sins and providing a way to You now and throughout eternity. In Jesus' name, amen.

Questions:

What did God speak to your heart as you read this story?

There are no coincidences for us in Christ. The Bible says in Ephesians 1:11 (NIV), "In him we were also chosen, having been predestined according to the plan of him who works out everything in conformity with the purpose of his will." Do you believe this to be true? If so, why?

What does Easter mean to you and what are some ways you recognize Christ on this holiday?

How has God reached out and comforted you in a profound way?

A Step Closer:

Here are some Bible verses related to God preparing us: Ezekiel 38:7, John 14:3, Proverbs 21:31, Ephesians 2:10, Psalm 23:5, Exodus 23:20, 2 Timothy 2:21, and 1 Peter 1:13.

Take a moment to write down the whole chapter of Psalm 23. Read it slowly, thanking God after each stanza and let it fill you with comfort and peace.

27

HEAVENLY HUGS

As I knelt down on the living room floor, cleaning out a nightstand for my daughter to use, I wiped down the outside and opened each drawer to take out the unused stationery. My heart was heavy over the things I was dealing with. I didn't mention it to anyone except Jesus. I was feeling overwhelmed and downhearted. I had spent the day trying to gather all the items my second daughter Olivia needed for college and watched as she drove away. I was already missing her.

Nevertheless, I continued cleaning out the nightstand for my baby girl, Priscilla, to place in her room she had spent hours cleaning. She plopped on the couch next to where I was. I smiled at her, feeling refreshed, as she brought such a peace with her that she was unaware of. Priscilla snuggled up on the couch and mentioned that she might like to take a little nap. I agreed and told her to go right ahead.

As I opened the last drawer of the nightstand, I grabbed a handful of our Christmas cards that we had printed too many of. As I placed them on the floor, a letter addressed to me from my mother fell out of the stack. It read:

Hello, my sunshine,

I pray you will make it through the day after such a long night. I know lights will be out early tonight. Thank you for getting Livi's birthday present. I'm looking forward to the day I can hug you again.

Love,

Mom

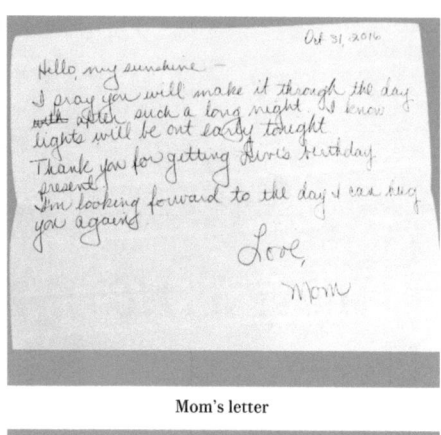

Mom's letter

Looking up at Priscilla, I handed her the letter and began to cry. She read it, dropped her jaw in awe, and hugged me, saying how sweet it was. I told her it was a gift given to me directly from God at the perfect moment.

I took a walk outside, held up my hands, and thanked God for loving me so much and for knowing exactly what I needed and gifting me with what felt like a hug from my mom. I had not told anyone how I was feeling that day, yet He knew. It was as if He was saying to me, "Daughter, I know. I am here with You. Here is a little something that will brighten your day … just because I love you."

One of my favorite verses in the Bible is found in Romans 8:38–39 (CSB). "For I am persuaded that neither death nor life, nor angels nor rulers, nor things present nor things to come, nor powers, nor height nor depth, nor any other created thing will be able to separate us from the love of God that is in Christ Jesus our Lord." This is precisely how I felt when fumbling upon those loving words written by my mom years ago. I told Priscilla that no one could convince me that God's love is not real.

God knew I was struggling emotionally, and He changed all that by handing me a treasure I had not even realized I had. In doing this, the heaviness of my heart dwindled. My heart was now glad. How loving of our Heavenly Father! I continue to be amazed by His attention to detail in our lives. He is the Creator of our universe, yet we must not forget that He is also our Father who cares about everything we are going through.

I carry the letter with me in my Bible as a reminder. A reminder of how excited I was to have found the letter from my mom and not remembering what was written in it, but knowing that when I opened it and read her words, somehow or another, I was going to be filled with love. I carry the letter in my Bible because it also serves as a reminder that the Bible is God's Word, His love letter to us. May we be just as eager to open and read it and accept the hope and love He has placed in there for us.

Prayer:

Thank You, Lord Jesus, for being the kind of Father who takes time out to hold our hands while we are trudging through the muck in life. Thank You for uplifting our sadness and replacing it with joy. What a Friend we have in You! In Jesus's name, amen.

Questions:

What thoughts or emotions rose up as you read this story?

What are you struggling with emotionally right now that you haven't shared with anyone? Trust that God knows, and He knows how to meet you exactly where you are and help you. You only need to ask Him.

In what ways do you *know* that Jesus is your friend? Do you feel His presence with you?

Do you believe God is paying attention to the details in your life? Why or why not?

A Step Closer:

Where in the Bible can you find a story or passage that shows Jesus taking a bad or sad situation and turning it into a good one? Here are a few stories to help you out: Ruth and Naomi found in the book of Ruth. Joseph's life story is found in Genesis. Daniel's journey is found in the book of Daniel (one of my favorite stories).

Here are some Bible verses pertaining to letters in the Bible: 2 Thessalonians 2:15, Hebrews 13:22, 2 Chronicles 2:11, 2 Chronicles 21:12, Isaiah 39:1, Jeremiah 29:1, and Acts 15:23–31.

Open your Bible today and ask God to "hug" you and fill you with His love as you read His Word.

28

Farewells

As we were driving in the night through the mountains of North Carolina, the street lights lit up the inside of the van every so often, allowing us to quickly see each other. At one point, my brother, sister and I caught a glimpse of my Maw Maw and shrieked, then burst out into laughter. To prank us, she waited until the streetlight shone on her and then dropped her false teeth down and smiled really big at us. We all laughed and laughed. She was a hoot.

Proverbs 17:22 (ESV) says, "A joyful heart is good medicine." My Maw Maw was blessed with the gift of laughter, making others laugh as well as often laughing at herself. Sometimes, what she chose to make us laugh about was appropriate, and sometimes, it wasn't. Nevertheless, she loved Jesus to the core and understood that He wants us to be joyful and playful and to enjoy life. I asked her one time, "Maw, how are you and Paw still so happy after all these years of marriage?" Her response was, "Well, Cheri, I know that Paw loves to laugh. And I know how to keep him laughing."

Toward the end of Maw Maw's life, she was in and out of the hospital. One time, I went to visit her and asked how she was feeling. She said, "Well, I guess God don't want me. I've given Him many chances to go ahead and take me, and here I am still on this side of heaven."

The last time I saw her was on my way to cheer/dance at an NFL Saints alumni game. Pippy practiced with me and knew the dance I was to perform, so I asked her if she wanted to show the dance to Maw Maw. There sat Maw Maw in the hospital room, clapping enthusiastically and laughing all the while as she watched

Pippy and I perform. That was my last memory of her—smiling, laughing, and cheering us on.

Weeks later, when it was time for her to go to heaven, family gathered around her, comforting her as she lay in the hospital bed. The doctors told the family members to go ahead and say their goodbyes to Maw Maw. Now, what you must understand is that this was during football season ... on a Saturday night ... in Baton Rouge, Louisiana. Although the room was filled with sniffles and sobs as everyone was saying their farewells, the football game was on and could faintly be heard.

My siblings leaned over, kissed Maw Maw, and repeated what most were saying, "It's okay, Maw, you can go on to heaven and see Jesus." Maw Maw slightly opened one eye and said, "What's the score?" Everyone laughed at her being halfway gone and still wanting to know if the Tigers beat 'Bama! It is so fitting that some of her last words made everyone laugh.

Farewells are not always so heavy and sad. Yes, we will have days filled with grief that seems unbearable. However, we all knew that Maw Maw loved Jesus and lived for Him, so we had no doubt in our minds we would see her again. I cannot help but smile when I think of Maw Maw and all the laughter she brought us. One thing I learned from her was to enjoy this life God has blessed us with.

John 16:33 (ESV) says, "In the world you will have tribulation. But take heart; I have overcome the world."

There will be hardships, no doubt, but roll with it, knowing that Jesus holds us through it all. And find reasons to laugh and share that laughter with your loved ones.

To answer Maw Maw's last question of what's the score ... it's touchdown Jesus! He wins!

Prayer:

Dear Lord Jesus, Thank You for allowing us to be on Your winning team. Thank You also for giving us joy and laughter throughout life. May we have a light heart as we keep our eyes focused on You instead of staying bogged down with the problems of the world. Help us remember that You want us to have fun while enjoying each other here on earth. In Your name we pray, amen.

Questions:

What memory came up for you as you read this story?

Do you have someone in life who makes you laugh just by the thought of them? Take a moment and thank God for them and the laughter they bring you.

Can you explain the verse Proverbs 17:22 (CSB) that "a joyful heart is good medicine"? Do you have examples in your life of this verse proving to be true?

Do you know that if your loved ones (who have passed away) accepted Christ they are in paradise in the presence of Jesus? When we are missing them, we can stop and think about where they are and give thanks to Jesus for allowing them eternal peace and joy.

A Step Closer:

Here are some Bible verses describing heaven: Isaiah 25:8–12, Matthew 5:17–20, Matthew 7:13–15, Luke 13:29–33, John 14:2–4, Revelation 7:13–17, and Revelation 21:4–8.

Here are some Bible verses pertaining to joy: Romans 15:13, Romans 12:12, Philippians 4:4, James 1:2, Galatians 5:22, John 16:24, and Proverbs 17:22.

My precious Maw Maw waving goodbye to us.

29

COUNTING

AFTER AN EVENING SPENDING time together with dinner and a movie, we savored a long hug and a sweet kiss. While still hugging, Brett would say a number to me. The first time he did this, I asked him what that number was. He said, "The number of minutes until I get to see you again." With a smile on my face, I walked over to my little red car and drove all the way back to Baton Rouge.

And sure enough, within the number of minutes Brett quoted me, I would be back on my way to see him again. When I drove up to his house, he was sitting on the doorstep, smiling and patiently waiting for me. These are the things that made me fall in love with that big, strong, handsome man.

As eager as we were as a young couple, counting down the minutes until we could be together again, I think about God's love for us and how much deeper it must be. It's hard to imagine (in fact, we are unable to imagine) just how much He loves us. The Bible says in Psalm 36:5 (ESV), "Your steadfast love, O Lord, extends to the heavens, your faithfulness to the clouds."

Another thing that fascinates me about the Lord is that He knows the very number of hairs on our heads. How precious we must be to God for Him to pay attention to us in such detail to count our hairs. It says in Matthew 10:30 (ESV), "But even the hairs of your head are all numbered." Think about that for a moment. Most people lose anywhere from 50 to 100 hairs a day. Of course, the number can vary for many different reasons. But my point is, no matter what time of day it is or if a hair just fell off my head, God still knows the exact number of hairs that are on my head. That means He is constantly paying close attention to us individually.

Psalm 139:1–6 (ESV) says, "O Lord, you have searched me and known me! You know when I sit down and when I rise up; you discern my thoughts from afar [...] and are acquainted with all my ways. [...] Such knowledge is too wonderful for me; it is high; I cannot attain it." He not only knows our exterior, but our interior. He knows our thoughts. He knows our hearts. And He still loves us. Does this not draw you to Jesus? The loving acts Brett did and still does for me draw me closer to him. The more we understand God's love for us, the more we are drawn closer to Him. The more we know about Jesus's character, the more we understand that He is safe to trust. And with Him, our hearts will be handled with loving care.

We recently watched a home video of when I had my third daughter, Shilah. The video was of my big girls getting to see and hold their baby sister for the first time. Everything Shilah did amazed the sisters. Olivia would jump in excitement and awe at any grunt or movement Shilah made. At one point in the video, Cora asked, "Can I hold Shilah again?" I answered, "In just a minute, I will let you hold her." Immediately, Cora started saying her ABCs, because that is how we measured minutes at that point in their lives. It was darling of Cora to want those minutes to pass so quickly that she began the countdown at once.

I am quite sure her enthusiasm mirrors how Jesus is with us every day. May we be just as eager to spend time with Him as the sisters were to hold Shilah, or how my husband was to see me. And may our love for Him be just as precious and treasured.

How often is Jesus sitting on the steps waiting for us to come to spend time with Him? How often has He begun the countdown of when we will set time aside for Him in prayer or just sit in His presence? How many ABCs has He already said?

Prayer:

Dear Lord Jesus, thank You for being eager to spend time with us. Thank You for loving us so much that You pay attention to every detail regarding each of us. May we long to spend time with You every day. We welcome You into our every moment in our days and in our lives. In Your precious name we pray, amen.

Questions:

What did God speak to your heart as you read this story?

James 4:8 (ESV) says, "Draw near to God, and he will draw near to you." In what ways do you know this verse to be true?

Go to God in prayer now and just spend time enjoying His presence.

A Step Closer:

Read Psalm 103:11–12 and then search for other verses in the Bible that confirm God, our Creator, longing to spend time with you.

Here are a few Scripture verses to help you start a journey of seeking Christ: Psalm 27:8, John 15:4, Psalm 42:1, Mark 1:35, Psalm 1:2, and Isaiah 40:31.

Shilah holding baby Priscilla.
She adored her new baby sister.

30

THE TUNNEL

NO MATTER IF ALL the kids are sleeping at this part of our drive to Florida, when we approach the tunnel, all of them wake up. We each roll the windows down, honk the horn, and start yelling, "Yay!" and "Woohoo!" The tunnel itself isn't what stirs happiness inside us. It's what awaits us on the other side.

Even as a child, I remember doing the same exact thing with our family when we went through the tunnel. Every summer we drove to the beautiful Florida beaches together. What awaited us on the other side was pure fun ... vacation time, the beach, hours spent in the sunshine, and playing in the sand. I remember my father holding me as we jumped the waves, swimming on rafts out to the sand bar with my siblings to look for seashells, building sandcastles, and running to Mom on the picnic blanket to eat the delicious lunch she had made for us to enjoy.

My kids have even deeper connections on the other side of the tunnel because of friends who, somewhere along the way, have become family. Friends they made memories with throughout the years by paddle boarding in the bay, jet skiing to the sand dunes, after-dinner games, and lots of late-night talking in the hot tub. There is also the beach, surfing, parasailing, sleepovers, sunshine, and tanning. All the fun stuff that makes these trips memorable.

God blesses us each with people to do life with. People who will encourage you to grow in Him. We have celebrated the highs and lows in life with our Florida friends and know we will continue to do so until we are all together in heaven. Even then, we will recognize our loved ones; the Bible says in 1 Thessalonians 4:17 (ESV), "Then we who are alive, who are left, will be caught up *together* with them in the clouds to meet the Lord in the air, and so we will always be with the Lord."

One day, we each will approach the tunnel that ends life's journey here on earth. Those of us who have accepted Christ as our Lord and Savior *know* what awaits us on the other side. In John 8:12 (ESV), Jesus says, "I am the light of the world. Whoever follows me will never walk in darkness, but will have the light of life." We will meet the Light of the world, Jesus, and we will be reunited with our Christian loved ones who will joyfully celebrate our arrival. As the old hymn goes, "When we all get to Heaven, what a day of rejoicing it will be. When we all see Jesus, we'll sing and shout the victory!"

As happy as we are to go see our Florida friends on the other side of the tunnel, how much happier we will be to reach our final destination with the One who loves us unconditionally. He is on the other side of the tunnel cheering us on to turn toward Him and walk the path that eventually leads to Him.

John 1:5 (NLT) says, "The light shines in the darkness, and the darkness can never extinguish it." May we not have tunnel vision by getting bogged down with our earthly troubles, but may we expectantly look ahead and walk towards the path that leads to Jesus, the Light at the end of the tunnel.

Prayer:

Thank You, Lord Jesus, for being the Light that guides us through life. Thank You, also, for God-given friendships that last throughout eternity. May we praise You as we enjoy the outside world like the beach and the mountains and all in between. Most importantly, may we each submit our lives to You, in order for true enjoyment and eternal peace to never end. In Your name, we pray, amen.

Questions:

What came up for you as you read this story?

What God-given friends do you have to enjoy life with?

How do you make time to seek the Light of the world daily? By doing so, you will keep on the right path that leads to eternal life.

A Step Closer:

Revelation 5:11 (NASB) says, "Then I looked, and I heard the voice of many angels around the throne and the living creatures and the elders; and the number of them was myriads of myriads, and thousands of thousands." Does this verse excite you? What other verses in the Bible excite you about meeting Jesus one day? Write them down and read them often, keeping your focus on heaven above.

Here are some Bible verses about Jesus being the Light: John 9:5, John 9:1–41, 2 Corinthians 4:6, Matthew 5:14–16, 1 John 1:1–10, and Revelation 22:5.

Driving through the tunnel headed to Florida.

Last Word for the Reader

If there is any point throughout your reading that you would like to shift the control over your life to Jesus and accept Him as your Lord and Savior, this following prayer will help you embark upon that important journey:

Jesus, I recognize that I am a sinner and in need of a Savior. I believe You are the Son of God and came into this world to show us how to live and that You died for my sins. I believe You resurrected and now are seated at the right hand of Your Father. Please forgive me of my sins and come into my heart and help me live for you. Thank You for this eternal gift of salvation. Jesus, it's in Your name I pray, amen.

If you have just said the above prayer and have welcomed Jesus into your heart, congratulations! I encourage you to open your Bible every day and read His Words to you. Ask the Holy Spirit to guide you every step of the way. And remember, He will never leave you, He loves you, and there is nothing you can do to take that love away. Enjoy the peace that comes from growing close to Jesus!

How This Book Was Birthed

ROCKING IN THE GLIDER as I nursed my baby girl, Priscilla, the Lord placed on my heart two things … that I was going to lead a Bible study and write a book. I was taken aback, considering I just had my fourth child and was a full-time homeschooling mom. After I placed Priscilla in her crib to sleep for the night, I went to our bedroom and told Brett what God had placed on my heart. I thought he would think it was interesting and maybe agree that it was puzzling information to take in. However, he immediately agreed. He confidently said, "Yes! That would be great!"

The first part of what God pressed upon my heart that evening while nursing my baby girl, was that I would lead a Bible Study. In no way at that time was I confident to take on such a task. After I moved to Texas and attended the Cowboy Wives Bible Study for many years, the leader moved away. Before she left, she asked if I, along with another wife, would take over and lead the group. It did not dawn on me until a couple of years into leading that I remembered what God told me so long ago. His words came to fruition in my life, and I was amazed. The other wife and I still lead the study and enjoy the blessing of fellowship and prayer time with the precious groups of ladies each football season.

I held what God had told me in my heart about writing for close to fourteen years. Along the way, I wrote a few things down here and there, not really knowing what I was supposed to be writing. I often approached God, saying, "God, I am not sure what I am doing here. Who would want to read my stories? I don't know how to go about this." His response to me was always, "You just write. I will provide the rest."

I never had specific ideas about what I was going to write. God would just place a general idea or word on my heart that triggered a memory from my past, then, He gave me a Scripture verse that coaligned with my story. I sat down before I wrote about it and asked God to breathe life into my story. He is the One who gave me each word. I continually prayed that not even one word would make it into my book that did not come from Him. God pressed upon me that as long as I am obedient to Him and do what He has called me to do, which right now is continuing to write, then He will be the One to supply *all* my needs. I need not worry about anything! He is faithful and will take care of me and my family. The Bible says in Philippians 4:19 (CSB), "And my God will supply all your needs."

I continue to be amazed at Him using me in such a way that brings me joy. Who would have ever thought ... I love to write! I love being open to allowing Him to relay messages through my life stories in order to draw others near to Him.

One thing God highlighted to me while writing this book was all the times "in Him" or "in Christ" was written in the Bible. So many good things come to fruition while being cultivated "in Him." John 16:33 (CSB) says, "I have told you these things so that in me you may have peace. You will have suffering in this world. Be courageous! I have conquered the world." Let's look at what the Bible verse says. It says that in the world, we will have suffering. But in Him, we will have peace. Without Him, we are miserable and lost. Our lives can seem worthless. However, in Him, we are worthy and loved, and our lives have purpose.

Thus, in Him, I will continue to be obedient to what He is asking me to do. I will hold the pen as He authors whatever else He wants to author in my life from here on out. I need only to trust *in Him* and obey.

Acknowledgments

To my Savior Jesus Christ! *All* glory be to You! Thank You for trusting me to share Your love with everyone who reads this book. Nothing I am or amount to is worth anything without You. May You always be my focus and may I always thirst for You.

To my husband, **Brett**, whom I call 'Buddy.' Our love story first started out with me being your cheerleader, and although I still am and always will be your cheerleader, you have become *my* biggest cheerleader. You are my steady love and my patient stronghold in life. My journey with you and our little ladies is what makes up so much of this book. I have been grateful for every second of being your wife and their mother. You were the first person I told so long ago about God wanting me to write this book. Thank you for confirming to me right then and there that you believe He chose me to write this. My prayer for you, Brett Lamar, is for God to bless you double-fold for all you have poured into my life. Thank you for grabbing my hand all those years ago. I love you endlessly.

To my darling daughters, **Cora**, **Olivia**, **Shilah**, and **Priscilla** (Pippy). You girls constantly encouraged me and prodded me to write regardless of insecurities that may have surfaced for me. Being alongside each of you throughout every stage of your life has been my greatest joy. I continue to marvel over you individually and thank God for the bond you share amongst each other that shines His love. Psalm 133:1 says, "Behold, how good and pleasant it is when brothers dwell in unity." I am the little lady who will forever be following you girls and cheering you on in life. You each bring something unique to our family that is priceless, and that binds us together so tightly. You girls are my heart, and I am eternally grateful to God for letting me love you, be your mother, *and* your friend.

To my **brother**. Throughout my entire life, you believed in me. Because of that, I have been able to experience so much. Thank you for always encouraging me to do my very best and rise above in all situations. Your love and support for my family and me have launched us into unimaginable places. I am so grateful for you. I am proud of you, and I love you.

To my **sister**. Thank you for introducing me to Christ when I was just ten years old, for teaching me how to read, and most of all, for reading the Bible to me and making it come alive. Thank you for encouraging me in my homeschool journey and in motherhood, as well. I love you.

To my **cousins**, my **nieces**, my **nephews**, my family and friends. Thank y'all for reading so many of my stories and giving me true feedback that helped me shape each chapter. May God bless each of you.

To **Victor** and **Eileen Marx**, you two are so inspirational to all who know and follow you. You lead the way to Christ with laser focus and warrior grit. I am honored to know you and cheer you both on in life as you continue to be champions! May God continue to bless your love and your ministry (ATP Ministries).

To my **Bible study ladies**. Thank y'all for letting me share my chapters when they applied to what we were learning. Thank y'all for praying for me. Our bond is eternal.

To my publishers, **Andrea**, **Lyneta**, and **Ruth**. Thank you each for taking a chance on me. Your wealth of wisdom helped me every step of the way. I could not have done this without your dedication and guidance.

To **Kanika Evans**. Thank you for your friendship throughout the years. I feel you and I are living similar lives, running this race for Jesus as we pour every ounce of love into our husband and children. And every now and then we glance over at each other and give a nod of respect and recognition. May God bless you endlessly for everything you do in His name and for His glory. Love you always.

ACKNOWLEDGMENTS

To **Katie Kane**. You are a genuine gift to me straight from God. He plopped you into my life like dropping a blessing directly down from heaven so long ago, yet you continue to brighten my life. You are more than a conqueror. Scholve.

To **Mrs. Carol Weber**. You have continuously shown Christ's love to me ever since the day we met. The very thought of you makes me thank God for placing you in my life. I love you.

To **Jessica Wuerffel**, you were my first friend in the NFL and definitely my first friend to motivate me to write this book. I don't think you know the words "I can't." You are a way maker, my friend. Thank you for helping me in the early stages and cheering for me throughout the entire process of this journey, as well as in life itself.

To **Natasha**, you not only read everything I sent your way, but you have been trekking through life with me almost daily for the past twelve years. You have been a constant friend who brings such grace and comfort to me. You are truly treasured.

To **Jenn, Carri, Lisa**, and **Fran**. Y'all are my circle and have become family to not only me but to my girls, as well. Thank you for praying for us and inspiring us continually. We love you each, as well as your precious families.

To **Mrs. Barbara Marinelli**, you have listened and helped guide me from the beginning of this project and you have surrounded me with love and genuine friendship for years now. I appreciate you so very much.

To **Randi**, my first friend editor (haha)! You are such an encouragement. You are selfless, driven, a powerful prayer warrior and loved by everyone. Most of all, you are a sister in Christ! I see you, girl!

To **Shelli Strickland** and **Tara Lay**, you both played an integral part in obediently pointing me in the right direction to make the thought of my book become a reality. Thank you and may God shower both you and your families with countless blessings.

To **Shelbi** and **Morgan**, thank you for letting me read my stories aloud to you. I needed to hear honest feedback from people other than close friends and family members. Your responses helped me more than you know. I deeply appreciate you both.

To all of you in my life, I am honored to know each one of you, and I hope y'all know how very loved you are not only by me but by our Savior Jesus.

Last but certainly not least, I want to acknowledge my late parents and grandparents, who now reside with Christ. I am who I am because of their leadership and prayers throughout my life. I deeply miss each of them but am overjoyed we will get to spend eternity together.

... and to my dog, **Roux**. Thank you for keeping my feet warm while I pecked away at the keyboard.

My lovely ladies I have so often written about in
the pages you have read.
Priscilla, Olivia, Shilah, and Cora

My Daddy
(Baton Rouge Police Department)

My beautiful Mama holding Shilah.

Cheri (7th grade)

IMAGES

Katie, my brother (Perley), and me
(Destin, Florida)

My cousins (Cheryl and Leisha),
my Maw Maw Jackson and me

Brett as a rookie NFL New Orleans Saints

The newspaper article advertising the event where Brett and I first met.

This picture was taken on that very day Brett and I met at the autograph signing.

Fran and Cheri (NFL alumni game 2019)

Brett and Cheri 2022

Olivia, Priscilla, Shilah, Cora

Cora, Olivia, Brett, Priscilla and Shilah
(Dallas Cowboys training facility)

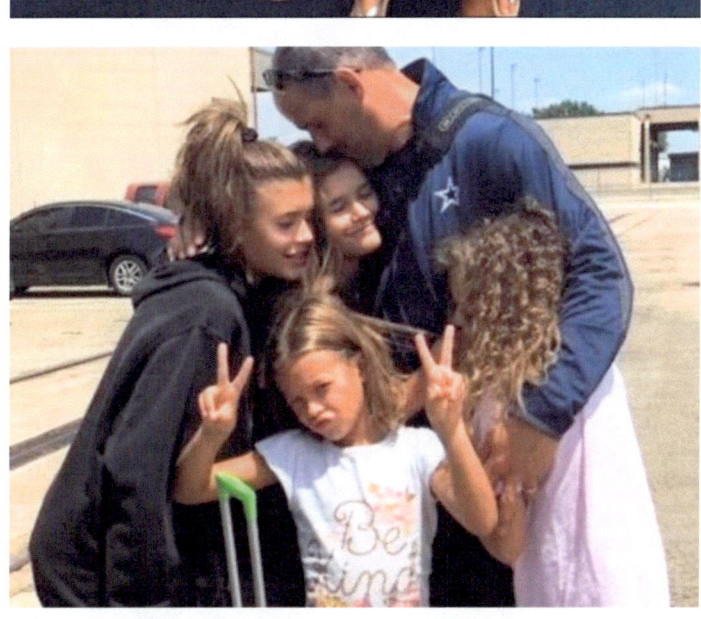

Olivia, Cora, Brett, Priscilla and Shilah
(Dallas Cowboys football training camp)

ABOUT CHERI BECH

CHERI JACKSON BECH IS a devoted follower of Christ with a deep desire to inspire others to seek a close and personal relationship with God. A wife, mother, and friend, Cheri approaches life with a tender heart and a passion for sharing her faith through real-life stories and devotionals. She knows firsthand the joys, challenges, and moments of grace that come with navigating faith and family, and she writes to connect with those who long to see God working in the everyday details of their lives.

As a former NFL cheerleader and NFL coach's wife, Cheri offers a unique and relatable perspective, finding ways to shine God's light in a world that often moves at a fast pace. She lives outside of Dallas and has been a homeschooling mom for her four daughters—Cora, Olivia, Shilah, and Priscilla (Pippy)—and cherishes the beauty of home, family, and community.

Cheri also leads Bible studies for NFL wives and girlfriends, following her calling to lift up other women on their journeys of faith. Her hope is that each devotion will offer encouragement, comfort, and a gentle reminder that God is always near, ready to walk alongside us. It is her prayer that through these pages, both men and women will find inspiration to draw closer to the One who loves them most.

Connect with Cheri at:
Email: cherijbech@gmail.com
IG: @cherijbech

Made in the USA
Columbia, SC
15 March 2025